I am privileged to look back on nearly seventy years of cricket. I have watched the game take on the shape of the world around it over and over again, and revelled in the friendship of so many men who have carried the torch of greatness through its history.

Cricket is a heritage, passed from generation to generation as a living, breathing thing . . . Each of the generations nurtures it, changes it a bit, and polishes it up for those who follow. I have been privileged, as a player and a broadcaster, to have been right in the thick of it for longer than most, and I have grown to respect the game, its traditions and its standards, as a reflection of all of life's good things.

I look back with joy. But I also look forward with confidence, in the clear belief that cricket will thrive, so that my children's children, and their children's children after them, will still be able to immerse themselves in the noblest of all games.'

Alan McGilvray, Captains of the Game, *1992*

McGILVRAY

THE VOICE OF CRICKET

A Tribute

EDITED BY NORMAN TASKER

an
ABC
BOOK

Published by ABC Books for the
AUSTRALIAN BROADCASTING CORPORATION
GPO Box 9994 Sydney NSW 2001

Copyright © Australian Broadcasting Corporation 1996

First published 1996

ISBN 0 7333 0490 7

Designed by Kaye Binns-McDonald
Set in 11/13 pt Times
by Midland Typesetters, Maryborough, Victoria
Printed and bound in Australia by Allwest Print, Perth, WA

5 4 3 2 1

CONTENTS

INTRODUCTION

W HEN ALAN McGILVRAY died in July, 1996, aged 86, a part of Australia seemed to die with him. An Australia of another time . . . a more tolerant, more patient, more straightforward time, when values were more certain and standards more identifiable. McGilvray would have been quite amazed at the outpouring of genuine sadness that his death triggered. The tributes flowed from people of all kinds . . . famous people whose lives had been touched through McGilvray's long career in radio, and just ordinary Australians for whom his voice was a sort of natural comfort through long summers of years past. Callers to ABC radio, in particular, spoke of McGilvray on the wireless as not mere cricket commentary, but as an integral part of the Australian summer . . . as a curiously intimate part of their growing up years. It was all the more remarkable for the fact that McGilvray had been retired from the airwaves for more than a decade, sufficient time for most in such a field to be well and truly forgotten.

Through half a century as a cricket commentator on ABC Radio, McGilvray had, indeed, become not only the voice of cricket, but the voice of summer. His warm, rich tones seemed to be the backdrop to everything through the hot months. For generations of Australians, young and old, it was there, along with the clickety-clack of the lawnmower, the hum of the cicadas, the rhythmic crashing of the waves on the beach. He was a constant . . . a symbol of a more relaxed era, when sport for sport's sake was a part of the Australian way of life, and standards of sportsmanship, of fairness, of right and wrong, were identified through sport as the hub of our ethos.

McGilvray had been a competent first-class cricketer himself, a contemporary of great names like Bradman, McCabe, O'Reilly. He had captained New South Wales, and he had developed through his own participation in the game a keen appreciation of everything it entailed . . . its players, its tactics, its ethics, its place in life. As a commentator he was able to share his insights and his understanding as perhaps no other commentator before or since. He knew his subject as few know it, and he had a capacity to communicate, in the most intimate way, that made whole generations of listeners feel as though they actually knew him. Those who did found him fascinating company.

McGilvray was adaptable to changing times, without ever compromising any of his standards of accuracy or impartiality, so that his work remained as powerfully respected in the 1980s as it had been in the 1930s.

This book represents a tribute to the life and times of Alan McGilvray, and the unique impact he had on broadcasting, on cricket and on the fabric of Australian life. The contributions from those who knew him—cricketers, broadcasters, journalists, political leaders—are complemented by the words of McGilvray himself, from the books he wrote upon his retirement from broadcasting.

Together, they leave no doubt as to his unique status as the voice of the endless summer.

POWER OF WORDS

by Gideon Haigh

*Gideon Haigh is a freelance journalist who has written
about sport, business and the arts for the* Age, the Australian *and the* Independent Monthly. *His first book,* The
Battle For BHP, *was published in September 1986.*

*Gideon has since written three books concerning
cricket—*The Cricket War—The Inside Story of Kerry
Packer's World Series Cricket *(1993),* The Border Years
(1994), and One Summer, Every Summer—An Ashes
Journal *(1995).*

GIDEON HAIGH

'Try and make the game better for your having been in it.' Such was
the advice the young Alan McGilvray received from his father when
selected to play for New South Wales 63 years ago. He never forgot
it. Over 50 years, his commitment and devotion to cricket was unques-
tioned. Generations grew to know him as Australia's semi-official
larynx of state. During summer, McGilvray commanded all ears,
calling the Test matches with imperturbable fairness and equity. And
during winter when Australia toured, his soothing tones were there
each morning to sum up our fortunes abroad.

McGilvrays emanate from Dumfries in Scotland, and Alan's
father Thomas arrived in Sydney as an infant in 1883. By the time
Alan David McGilvray was born in Birchgrove on 6 December 1909
as one of four children, Thomas had become proprietor of a city shoe
warehouse.

Monty Noble's Australians had just retained the Ashes in
England, and it was Noble who at Sydney Grammar School picked
out McGilvray as an all-rounder of promise. He went on to captain
the school First XI. While at school, McGilvray also attracted the help
of an elocution teacher who cured a schoolboy stammer and left him
with a clear, well-modulated voice.

Mac's great mentor, MA Noble. Noble was a fine Australian all-rounder at the turn of the century, and was arguably Australia's first great captain.

Alan worked alongside his brother Norman McGilvray at Thomas McGilvray & Sons after leaving school, while striving to impress New South Wales selectors, playing for both Paddington and Waverley. Alan Kippax led a fine state side at the time, which revolved on the axis of Don Bradman and Bill O'Reilly, so the call did not come until December 1933: days before his 24th birthday, McGilvray was taken to Adelaide Oval to be 12th man for the state's match against South Australia.

A fortnight later he was capped against Victoria. McGilvray made 11, batting briefly with Bradman (187 not out) before misreading the perplexing Chuck Fleetwood-Smith. He also dismissed Ben Barnett in the second innings, the only wicket to elude a rampant Bill O'Reilly (9 for 50).

McGilvray fared well enough that season to be mentioned in dispatches among the selectors choosing Bill Woodfull's 1934 Australian side, but it was another development associated with that trip that was to have greater bearing on his future.

* * * * *

It was the ABC's first general manager Harold Parkyn Williams who, in 1930, had conceived of broadcasts simulating cricket matches from England, with commentators expanding on coded cablegrams. But it was his successor Walter Tasman Conder who commissioned an ambitious subordinate called Charles Moses to make the idea a reality in time for the 1934 visit with the 'Synthetic Test' broadcasts.

Moses himself led a commentary panel featuring Noble, Clem Hill, Clarence ('Nip') Pellew, Ted a'Beckett and Oliver Wendell Bill

The first synthetic broadcasts in 1934 were major social occasions. Here well-dressed wives, parents and children of the Australian team gathered in the ABC Radio studio in Market Street, Sydney, to listen to the second day of the third Test from Old Trafford, Manchester.

at the ABC's Market Street studio which re-created the matches from cables composed by Eric Sholl.

The team assembled at 7.30 pm every evening to pore over preliminary messages about the state of the ground, the weather and the topography of the fielding positions, with which they embroidered their comments when the transmissions began an hour later. Gramaphone discs provided crowd noises, while the sound of bat on ball was imitated by the rap of a pencil on a hollowed hemisphere of wood.

The effect on a cricket-crazy nation as the broadcasts echoed through to 3.30 am was pronounced. Wireless sales leapt. Bars and cafes remained open round-the-clock so that customers could hang on every word. Families hosted all-night parties, where guests congregated round radio sets to catch every nuance of the play. Patronage at cinemas and theatres fell. Employers complained bitterly of workers arriving too fatigued to discharge their duties.

Australians, ironically, enjoyed much better coverage of the

A crowd gathered to listen to the synthetic broadcast of the fall of the last wicket in Australia's win over England in the first Test at Trent Bridge in 1934. Note Australia's incredible reliance on Grimmett and O'Reilly, who together bowled 85 out of 102 overs.

series than Britons. The BBC carried only two 10-minute commentaries a day. Yet 12 000 miles away, the ABC filled the night with continuous ball-by-ball descriptions.

Moses succeeded Conder as general manager with a strong belief that the power of sport could popularise his young medium, and was henceforward always keen to build his cadre of cricket expertise. And it was doubtless with this in mind that he contacted McGilvray in November 1935, with a view to the cricketer delivering close-of-play summaries of NSW's forthcoming match against Queensland at the Gabba.

McGilvray had by this time inherited the NSW captaincy, and was chary of doing anything that might raise the ire of the NSWCA. But he was persuaded by Moses' forceful advocacy and, notwithstanding a faltering beginning, continued the work until his omission from the NSW side in January 1937.

A word is necessary here of McGilvray's cricket abilities. He was left-handed and stylish with the bat, right-handed and astute with the ball at medium-pace. His first-class figures (684 runs at 24.4 and 20 wickets at 57 in 20 matches, a dozen as captain) do not proclaim a distinguished presence, but his analytical powers and close catching skills made him a serviceable first-class traveller.

McGilvray was noted most, in fact, for his tactical acumen, the most renowned example of which was a trap he laid for Bradman (then playing for South Australia) at the SCG in January 1936. Using the left-handed Bob Hynes, he induced a leg-slip catch by Ray Little: one of Bradman's 16 first-class ciphers.

Almost certainly, too, McGilvray was prematurely dispensed with: he was only 27 and would top the 1936–37 Sydney grade batting averages (having led the bowling averages in the previous season). But he did not protest—beyond suspecting that his embryonic broadcasting career might have influenced matters—for he had just married Gwendolyn Griffiths and reasoned that Thomas McGilvray & Sons probably merited closer attention.

Moses did not forget him, however, and McGilvray was again recruited when the ABC ran its 1938 'Synthetic Tests'. This was an even more ambitious program than in 1934, and was indeed the first attempt at a complete ball-by-ball synthetic coverage, with McGilvray joining Noble, Hal Hooker and Vic Richardson in Sydney translating the cablegrams of Sholl and Chester Wilmot (the 27-year-old captain of the Melbourne University debating team). After midnight, indeed, it was often possible for Sholl and Wilmot to be heard direct on short-wave from the UK.

Moses dictated that his men participate fully in the experience. They ate 'lunch' at 10.30 pm as though in England, and referred throughout to pictures of the relevant Test match grounds so that they could describe their key features to listeners. McGilvray described it as 'broadcasting as an art form' and 'a pioneering adventure that left no doubt where my future lay'.

* * * * *

The irony was, of course, that McGilvray did not see the country he was describing for another decade. Having accepted the invitation of Bernard Kerr to call the 1946–47 Ashes series in Australia with Arthur Gilligan and Victor Richardson, he arranged a working trip to England in 1948 for the family business that also allowed him time to work with the BBC as the ABC's representative.

McGilvray's recollections of his initial Test broadcast in England alongside Gilligan during the first Test at Trent Bridge intimate the awe with which the wireless was regarded, and the magic of the first long-distance broadcasts.

'Arthur joined me in the opening moments of the commentary and we spoke to Australia,' McGilvray wrote in the 1950–51 ABC Cricket Book. 'What a thrill it was. I was really nervous. As I left the microphone after my first 20 minutes' spell that empty feeling returned and I thought of all I had not done. Surely I spoke too quickly, forgot this and that, omitted to mention so and so. I anxiously awaited the cables that I knew my wife, family and friends would send me, giving their opinion of the reception. Strangely they were pleasing, so I gradually regained my confidence and felt a whole lot better after the first day, and really settled to my task.'

McGilvray was something of a novelty to English listeners— accustomed to plummy phrasing and rounded vowels—and the BBC subsequently invited him to give a radio talk on the culture of his Australian audience. 'I spoke of the nightly interest we people take in Test matches—of the homes and parties and generally how people lived whilst a Test match is being played in England,' McGilvray recorded. 'I generally found it difficult to convince the people of England that such things could happen.'

The BBC's John Arlott also made use of McGilvray's antipodean intonation by casting him in a radio program in July commemorating the centenary of the birth of Dr WG Grace. McGilvray put on his most nasal strine to recite the eulogies for Grace of former Test captain Billy Murdoch.

But curiously, considering that they were to be bracketed as the best in their craft, McGilvray and Arlott were destined for at best distant regard. Arlott deprecated McGilvray's unadorned fact-before-fancy technique, while McGilvray found the elegiac ramblings of Arlott and his partner Rex Alston inattentive to the basic tenets of broadcasting.

In David Rayvern Allen's biography of Arlott, in fact, McGilvray sounds one of the few dissonant sentiments about the subject: 'He was a good commentator in his own way, but he didn't give the score or the card. I mentioned this to him and he said: ''Who wants the score? I'm not interested in the score.'' You should give the score three times in every six ball over.'

Perhaps discord was inevitable between two such strong-willed men. Arlott produced poetry in his other guise at the BBC and was an intimate of Dylan Thomas. McGilvray was a former player from an organisation where Bernard Kerr once famously advised Michael Charlton: 'Just describe the game. Cut out the fancy bullshit.'

* * * * *

McGilvray answered cheerfully to the tag of a 'straight' broadcaster, and never sought to emulate the breezy rapport of, say, Gilligan and Richardson. He quoted the advice once given him by Charles Moses: 'Leave the jokes to Richardson. He's got a sense of humour.'

The poetic, picturesque touches of Arlott and Alston were not for him. There was a famous occasion at Lord's where Arlott filled a break for bad light with a solo description of the unfurling of the covers: a wonderful, playful piece of broadcasting whose spontaneous eloquence takes your breath away.

But McGilvray demonstrated that a straight path in broadcasting need not be a narrow one. He imbued with drama the simplest activity of a day's course, wringing from it every possible significance. For communicating the low-level drama of a tight Test match corner, he can hardly have been equalled.

Think of a defensive shot. Now imagine it the way the young McGilvray might have described it. 'Bedser to Morris, now, the bowler's long strides as he approaches umpire Barlow. Bowls just short of a good length and Morris goes part of the way back, pushing it out to extra cover where Compton skips to his left to field. Morris looks after the ball, as though it came off a little slower than he expected, and Bedser may have held that one back slightly for it struck low on the bat. He's a cunning bowler, this Englishman, and this has been a fine containing spell. The pitch has also been a little two-paced today. Morris would probably like to be driving those on the rise, but the ball is now 65 overs old and the bounce is a little inconsistent.'

Such assiduous description might have gilded the lily somewhat, but it involved the listener in every level of the struggle: batsman against bowler, player against himself, cricketer against conditions, captain against captain. The delivery was always low, almost *sotto voce*. Other commentators sometimes had to strain to catch that intimate whisper.

McGilvray's deployment of pauses—in which he was allegedly instructed by no less an orator than Robert Menzies—was at its most telling when a wicket fell or a boundary was struck. He became wonderfully adept at enlisting the crowd in the instant of dismissal. 'And he's caught by Chappell!' would come the urgent report, followed by a break to capture the audience tumult, then a crisp vignette of the bowler's triumph.

So subtle and nuanced was the McGilvray *modus operandi* that his style was actually very difficult to parody in the way that Billy Birmingham (The 12th Man) made merry of Channel Nine's gallery of experts. There were certain elliptical phrasings peculiar to McGilvray ('As well as it was bowled, so was it played'), but none that lent itself readily to satire.

* * * * *

McGilvray's attention to detail made him, in fact, the ideal foil for other broadcasters. During the 1950–51 Ashes series, he forged an outstanding broadcasting partnership with the former sports editor of the Sydney *Sun*, Alban George Moyes, better known by the epithet Johnny.

A free-scoring NSW batsman picked for the cancelled Australian tour of South Africa in 1914–15 and then disabled during the Great War, Moyes had an encyclopedic knowledge of the game and a broad, laconic, unfaltering delivery. PL Williams—the legendary cricket coach of Geelong College, Wesley College and Prahran—described him as 'Cricket's Arch-Priest, the Prophet of Doom, the Fountain of All Knowledge, his cricket erudition matched only by a sort of satanic power'.

Australia's captain against Freddie Brown's Englishmen that season, Lindsay Hassett, was to become another great McGilvray sidekick after Moyes died in 1963. Hassett was puckish, engaging and self-deprecating—avowing frequently that he would have hated to commentate on his own batting.

No broadcasting liaison since has approached their complementarity. Like an opening pair so familiar that they eschew calling, McGilvray and Hassett had an almost telepathic understanding. 'We had an affinity that meant we could get to the heart of any issue quickly,' McGilvray once explained. 'We knew each other's minds.'

* * * * *

McGilvray actually spent a good deal of the 1950s in commercial radio. When Bernard Kerr accompanied the Australian team to England in 1953 for the ABC, he anchored a studio show on the Tests in Sydney for 2UW. When Michael Charlton accompanied the 1956 side, McGilvray was his competitor for 2UE.

McGilvray was accompanied on that trip by his wife Gwen— one of the few occasions on which she was able to do so—and there were always family considerations for McGilvray in accepting overseas trips.

Son Ross had been born in 1938, followed by daughter Carolyn in 1943, and the young family were obliged to accept cricket's dominion. 'When he was overseas for three and four months at a time, my mother missed him terribly,' says Carolyn Butler nee McGilvray. 'He was a real man of the house . . . I also remember the way we used to finish our Christmas lunches early, because my father would have to be on a plane to Melbourne for the Boxing Day Test the next day.'

The daily diet of cricket chat at the McGilvray home in Vaucluse did not, however, prove toxic. 'We had cricket for breakfast, lunch and dinner when we were growing up,' Carolyn recalls. 'We thought that everyone did because, when you grow up with someone, you don't know any differently. We certainly never thought of him as a celebrity. To us he was just a wonderful father.'

McGilvray returned to the ABC in time to call the high-rolling 1960–61 Australia v West Indies series. It was a heady season, still regarded as the most compelling of the post-war period, and McGilvray was at his best in graphing its see-sawing fortunes.

McGilvray missed, however, the crowning moment of the summer: the first tie in Test cricket history at the Gabba on 14 December 1960. Believing at lunch that the match was destined to dawdle to a draw, he decided to take an early flight back to Sydney with Keith Miller and leave the last rites to Charlton, Moyes and the ABC's Queensland sporting supervisor Clive Harburg.

Harburg it was who called that breathless last over, and McGilvray rued his decision as 'the greatest error of judgement in my

9

life'. Henceforward he never left a Test early, draining each match to the lees rather than miss a moment's drama.

When Thomas McGilvray & Son was sold in 1961, McGilvray's duties at the ABC expanded. Moyes' death had left a vacancy in the editing of the ABC Cricket Book which Moses had founded in 1934 and, after journalists Eddie Kann and Ern Christensen edited editions, McGilvray took over the pocket dossier and ran it for 25 numbers over 30 years. At the time he was placed on an exclusive contract with the ABC which made him the automatic choice for future tours.

McGilvray's pithy pen pictures and the statistics that he compiled manually made it indispensable. As surely as Wisden's yellow cover in April proclaims the beginning of the new English season, the ABC's popular periodical has come to announce the commencement of cricket hostilities here.

*   *   *   *   *

One of McGilvray's most notable characteristics as a commentator was his sense of Australianness. Though never partisan, he was resolutely patriotic where Australian teams were concerned. As former Australian vice-captain Keith Stackpole says: 'When Alan was commentating, you always felt that he was with you. Although he never let it get in the way of the fairness of his commentating, he was always an Australian: he was happy when you won, and he always suffered when you were beaten.'

McGilvray was often seen round the nets before a Test match, watching and occasionally offering help. He tutored Neil Hawke in the perfecting of a slower ball, counselled Ian Chappell in matters of captaincy, and New South Welshman Brian Booth remembers a lean trot cured by McGilvray's powers of observation.

'I was having a bit of a run of outs and Alan came up to me one day and said: ''When you were batting well you always seemed to have a lot of time. Now you seen to be hurrying a bit. It might be that you're picking your bat up too late. Try and make an effort to start your back-lift as the bowler's letting it go''. It was very good advice and it's something I pass on when I'm coaching kids now.'

On a few occasions the advice was more personal. Queenslander Peter Burge had suffered a wretched run of outs leading up to the Leeds Test of 1964, and admitted to McGilvray that he was anxious about his place in what shaped as the decisive match of the series.

The evening before the game, McGilvray appeared at his hotel room door with a bottle of scotch. The pair steadily drained it as

After he had passed through a lean period, Brian Booth, a talented Australian batsman of the 1960s, credited Mac with giving sound advice on the timing of his backlift.

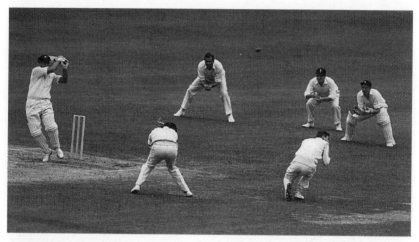

Queenslander Peter Burge made 160 against England at Old Trafford in 1964—an innings described by Mac as one of the greatest ever played. Here Burge pulls Trueman for a boundary.

McGilvray listened to Burge pouring out his sorrows, and the commentator left the bottle behind when he went to bed. A few days later Burge wrested the initiative from England with a devastating 160 that won the match and, in due course, the rubber.

In distant climes, and before the age of fax and cellular phone, McGilvray was often an avenue of communication between players and loved ones. Bill Jacobs, who managed Australian teams in South Africa in 1966 and the West Indies in 1973, recalls McGilvray arranging to deliver Grahame Thomas news of the birth of his baby in Sydney while the Australians were playing at Kimberley.

When Bill Lawry and Keith Stackpole suffered head wounds in Durban and Port-of-Spain respectively, McGilvray broadcast reassuring messages for anxious relatives at home.

'He was a top companion on tour, Mac, very good value,' says Jacobs. 'Two great things about him: he never invaded the dressing room; he could have but he didn't. And he always bought a drink. Some press guys will turn up to functions and drink all your booze, but never buy a round. Mac always did, or he'd invite you up for a drink in his room.'

There are legion stories of McGilvray's liberal out-of-hours hospitality and, indeed, his cast iron constitution. Alan Davidson recalls a morning before an Adelaide Oval Test match when he and co-selector Ray Lindwall accepted a McGilvray invitation to breakfast.

'Alan told us to come along to his hotel at 7.30 am,' Davidson recalls. 'So Ray and I knocked on his door and Alan says: "Don't worry. Breakfast's on the way."

'Anyway it gets to 7.40 am and there's no sign. And it gets to a quarter to eight and no-one's appeared. Then at ten to eight there's a knock at the door and in walks a waiter with a tray full of beers.'

* * * * *

McGilvray did not always take Australia's part. During the fifth Test against the West Indies at the SCG in January 1952, for instance, he was intensely critical of the intimidatory bowling that Lindwall and Keith Miller loosed upon the West Indian Everton Weekes.

Lindwall, usually the mildest of men, accosted him afterwards: 'You had no right to say those things. I ought to punch you in the nose.'

'Hit me and I'll fall down,' McGilvray replied. 'But I'll get up a gentleman and you won't be.'

In the West Indies in 1965, too, McGilvray could easily have sided with the patriotic consensus that Charlie Griffith had thrown Australia to defeat. He did not. Contra Sir Donald Bradman, Richie Benaud and especially captain Bob Simpson, McGilvray continued to express the unpopular view that Griffith's delivery was within the letter of the law.

McGilvray's was a bold stance that provoked harsh responses at home: at one stage, he feared that the ABC would recall him. But it earned McGilvray one of the compliments he most valued during his broadcasting career. Qantas chairman Sir Hudson Fysh wired him in the Caribbean, at the height of the slings and arrows, advising: 'We are all proud of your excellent summary given tonight, upholding the best traditions of sportsmanship.'

When the flak really flew, though, Australian cricketers learned to depend on McGilvray's fortitude and commitment to calling events as he saw them. In May 1978, most famously, it fell to him to describe the riot at Sabina Park that truncated the fifth Test of a turbulent Australia–West Indies Test. The fuzzy wirephotos of the Australian team fleeing the arena under a blizzard of bottles only hint at the disorder of the day. McGilvray's electrifying broadcast—carried over the morning news bulletins with the sound of gunfire in the background—sticks fast in the collective memory.

So incendiary was the situation in Jamaica and so unequivocal

Ray Lindwall had one of the smoothest fast bowling actions in history and was the attacking spearhead of Bradman's famous 1948 side. Mac criticised him and Keith Miller for intimidatory bowling against the West Indies in 1952—an impartial judgment which drew Lindwall's ire.

McGilvray's descriptions of it, in fact, that he was taken into Australian government custody to ensure his safe passage out of the country at the conclusion of the match. A brave man, McGilvray.

* * * * *

By this time, McGilvray had truly become an Australian cricket icon. Though professionalisation and mass marketing was changing cricket unrecognisably, McGilvray was a still point in a moving world: matter-of-fact, unflappable and unerring.

Ironically he was about to become a creature of marketing himself, as the ABC sought to promote his talents through an advertising campaign that exhorted the public to 'Watch the Tests on ABC Radio.' Though really as superfluous as a promotional push for water, the slogan and jingle asserting that 'The Game Is Not The Same Without McGilvray' did alert Australians to his extraordinary endurance and the continuity of radio's most distinguished septugenarian.

The crowning moment of the campaign came before play on the first day of the third Test between England and Australia on 1 February 1980, when the MCG scoreboard was adjusted to register: 'McGilvray 100'. It was the 100th Test between the two oldest enemies that McGilvray had described, and the commentator was the subject of countless tributes from players, umpires and administrators.

Even the occasionally blimpish Englishman EW Swanton sang his praises in an article for the 1981 Wisden. '(But) for both quality and length of service, Alan McGilvray's career at the microphone stands alone,' he wrote. 'To the listeners of every Test match playing country he stands for generous-minded, unbiased, factual common sense. At any crucial moment of an England–Australia Test, the ideal recipe, for me, is to turn on the television picture, turn off the sound, and listen to Alan.'

It was around this time that, as an 11 or 12-year-old, I had a little to do with McGilvray. It started when he selected for the *National Times* his all-time Australian XI, based on the wisdom of more than four decades as a player and pundit. With my youthful irreverence I was inclined to differ with him.

I could not, to begin with, understand how he had omitted Victor Trumper in favour of Bill Ponsford. How could his team do without Trumper's legendary bad-wicket legerdemain, while including a batsman known to be suspect against express pace? The attack needed a left-armer, too: Bill Johnston or Alan Davidson, perhaps, ahead of Dennis Lillee. And I also challenged his choice of Sir Donald Bradman as a captain (ah, the follies of youth!). Surely Monty Noble was the only man for the job.

McGilvray, of course, was at the pinnacle of his profession. And my mother—having perused some of my more unvarnished sentiments—warned that I could scarce expect a reply.

Of course, I got one. It came barely a week later and—judging from the typing errors and biro corrections on Commission note-paper—had been personally tapped out. It was also, of course, the perfect reply: detailed and balanced and never condescending. It was difficult for him to judge Trumper having never seen him (he was old, he said, but not that old!). And he had enormous reverence for Noble, who'd so encouraged him as a player at Sydney Grammar during the 1920s and later commentated alongside him.

McGilvray thought my side 'hard to beat', and observed that argument about the composition of champion XIs was one of the happiest entertainments for watchers of 'our marvellous game'. He looked forward, moreover, to hearing from me again.

I didn't let McGilvray down—dashing off a number of letters about matters of cricketing moment over the next few years—and he never did me. His replies were always prompt, thoughtful and generous. It's only now with the apprehensions of age (I'm 30), that I wonder at both my own chutzpah and McGilvray's tolerance. But perhaps that is a mark of the man.

*   *   *   *   *

Though it is sacrilegious to say so, McGilvray may have been a little below par toward the end of his long tour of duty. After Hassett retired in 1982, he was unsettled by the lack of continuity in the ABC commentary ranks. And calling Test matches through 74-year-old eyes during his final Australian summer of 1984–85, he did seem at times to be calling from memory.

On his 10th trip to England in 1985 accompanying Allan Border's team, however, McGilvray seemed back to his best. Perhaps it was being away from the celebrity circuit, perhaps it was his clarity amid the cake-crazy frivolity of the BBC's 'Test Match Special', but he seemed remarkably poised once again. After the fifth Test at the Oval, he launched the first of three books of memoirs (*The Game Is Not The Same . . .*) written with Norm Tasker, which proved a satisfying and entertaining epilogue to his half century of broadcasting.

His death severs a link to an age of grace, when the game was all, every ball was red, helmets were for miners and deep-sea divers, and players drove Holdens and Fords. A great broadcaster, for sure. He also wrote a lovely letter.

Alan McGilvray fell into broadcasting in the summer of 1935–36, when he was captain of NSW and the ABC were making early attempts to establish a comprehensive and authoritative cricket coverage. McGilvray had been summoned by Charles Moses at the suggestion of the former Australian captain MA Noble, who had become something of a McGilvray mentor after first coaching him at Sydney Grammar School. In his book, The Game Is Not The Same, *McGilvray recalled his first radio experience:*

ALAN McGILVRAY

Charles Moses, later a knight of the realm and a long term general manager of the Australian Broadcasting Commission, was the first big influence on sports broadcasting in Australia. Moses was a tremendously keen sportsman himself, a first grade Rugby forward with the Eastern Suburbs club in Sydney and long-term president of that club. He loved sport, and as the head of sports broadcasting in the early days of the ABC, he was the first really to perceive what radio offered sport and, more particularly, what sport offered radio and what radio offered the sporting public.

It was a phone call from Moses that started it all for me. The NSW Sheffield Shield team was heading off to Brisbane. It was my first year as captain and we had been doing moderately well, considering the loss of people like Bradman and McCabe, and the necessary influx of young, relatively inexperienced players. Moses had started to gather a small army of former cricket greats to provide authority for the ABC cricket broadcasts. He was not the sort of man to do anything sloppily, and he believed if the ABC was to broadcast cricket credibly, it would have to use commentators who had been through the mill. He wanted people who knew what they were talking about, and whose names and obvious experience would give instant authority to whatever they said. Former Australian captains Vic Richardson and Monty Noble were making their names as cricket broadcasters, and I suspect it was Noble who first suggested me to Moses.

For that first Brisbane trip it was obviously a matter of convenience. I was there, I was the NSW captain, and on Noble's recommendation I knew something about the game and its

Victor Richardson was one of Australia's most versatile sportsmen and a pioneer cricket broadcaster with the ABC. He was probably Mac's greatest mate during his early years behind the microphone.

tactics. An end-of-day summary was a fairly harmless experiment anyway. I didn't know quite how to react to Moses' call. I had a suspicion the rather austere powers of the NSW Cricket

Association might look upon the State captain moonlighting as a cricket commentator as being a little avant garde for their conservative tastes. And I certainly did not want to take on anything that would detract from my performance as a NSW player and NSW captain.

But radio was an exciting new field in which to involve oneself, and Moses was a very plausible apostle of its value. 'Why not?' I reasoned. It seemed harmless enough, not terribly time-consuming, and an experience I undoubtedly would find interesting. Besides, I thought, it's only a one-off thing. Little did I realise!

I had to do that first report from a studio in Brisbane. I was asked to sit in front of a microphone and fix my eyes on a light on the wall. When the red light went off and the green came on I was to start my report. When the green went off, and the red came on, I was to wind up, quickly. The first part offered no real problem. The green light came on and away I went. The trouble was there was no way of anticipating when the red light would light up again, and I raced through what I had to say in not very long at all.

It was a very amateurish broadcast, but at least the substance of what I had to say was reasonable, even if the manner of saying it was not. But once I had said it, I had said it, and still the green light beamed down at me. I babbled on about anything that came into my head. Goodness knows how many times I repeated myself, or contradicted myself, but I was determined I would not be caught with my mouth open, speechless and without a thought, like a small boy, stage struck at the school concert.

That broadcast lasted only a few minutes, but to me it was seemingly endless. The green light burned down at me like the work of some sadistic sorcerer, and the babble of words poured from my mouth. By the time the red light released me from my torment, my mouth was dry and I had broken out in a panic-stricken sweat. But I had done it, and it was to prove the most significant few minutes of torment in my life.

Moses obviously thought me worth some perseverance, and I continued to do after-play reports throughout the rest of the season and into the next, when Gubby Allen's MCC tourists were in Australia.

As Gideon Haigh has pointed out, McGilvray was a prolific letter writer. He would have regarded it as gross discourtesy had he neglected to reply to those who took the time to write to him. In the second of his books, The Game Goes On, *he recounted the following exchange with a regular correspondent.*

There was a lady who wrote to me once and explained that she had worked out I had spoken over BBC radio in England alone something above twenty million words. She assessed that by assuming my speech to be about 160 words per minute and by multiplying that by the number of sessions I would do in the Tests I had broadcast. She took off two and a half per cent for rain and early finishes, and two and a half per cent for error. This left her somewhere around twenty million words.

I was intrigued by the trouble to which she had gone and the ingenious manner in which she had worked it all out. I turned the page and she announced the number of words she had tallied. 'And every one of them has been sheer rubbish,' she concluded. I corresponded with that elderly lady for years thereafter and her sense of humour somehow provided a down-to-earth perspective for me in the latter stages of my broadcasting career.

A WORLD OF CHANGE

by Bob Hawke

Bob Hawke was one of Australia's longest-serving Prime Ministers, occupying The Lodge from 1983 to 1991. He is also a lifelong cricket devotee, having played senior club cricket himself in his youth.

BOB HAWKE

I often wonder at what a different world this is from the one in which I grew up as a boy. This sense of wonderment at the magnitude of change that has occurred in our lifetime was best captured by an American sociologist who wrote some years ago: 'I was born in the middle of human history. The world today is as different from the world in which I was born, as that world was from Julius Caesar's.'

When I heard of Alan McGilvray's death these considerations came flooding into my mind in a very direct and personal way because he embodied the way these dramatic changes had impacted on one of my passions—the love of cricket.

In 1938, aged eight, I was living in Maitland, a small country town on the Yorke Peninsula in South Australia. My father, a Congregational minister, and my mother had gone off on a long caravan tour of the eastern states and, much to my delight, I was left in the care of a farming family, parishioners of my parents. My incessant requests for any or all of them to bowl to me had already left them in no doubt about my fanaticism for the game but they weren't quite ready for my request that I should be allowed to stay up late to listen to the broadcast of the Test matches from England.

So began my first experience as a negotiator. I acknowledged the importance of getting enough sleep and proposed that as soon as I got back from school I should have something to eat, go to sleep immediately and then be woken up to hear the broadcast for a few hours.

And so it was agreed ... and so began my admiration for Alan McGilvray. I had no idea of the elaborate means he and his colleagues were employing to establish an authentic atmosphere by re-creating the details of each over of play on the basis of cablegrams sent from the ground. The sound of bat on ball was a pencil tapped on the ABC desk in Sydney!

As far as the young boy in country South Australia was concerned, he was right there at the big game. I can still remember the agonising temerity of a precocious Len Hutton daring to challenge the Test record of my idol, Don Bradman. I was willing him to get out on every ball but it was not to be as he went on to his mammoth total of 364 at The Oval.

The magic that Alan McGilvray displayed in those early days never deserted him. As we all became accustomed to the marvels of real-time colour television coverage, I know that I was one of many who turned off the TV sound so that we could still get the benefit of his incomparable commentaries.

Alan brought to his task the perceptive and intimate knowledge of a first-class player and captain together with a generosity of judgment lacking in so many of his comtemporaries. And above all was that beautiful voice which he always ensured was well lubricated with an appropriate intake of his beloved Scotch whisky.

I had the opportunity of getting to know Alan personally in many encounters and, for me, he was always the essence of good-humoured charm and civility. His knowledge of the game and its players was encyclopedic and he was generous but unoppressive in sharing this with others.

My memories of this great Australian—commentator and ambassador for his country par excellence—will always be warm. But above all I will treasure the man who had given so much pleasure 58 years ago to the bleary-eyed young boy setting off in the horse and sulky to that remote little country school.

The synthetic Tests of 1938 were a marvel of pioneering broadcasting which Alan McGilvray always placed among the most exciting ventures he had ever been involved in. He regarded its inventiveness, its amazing improvisation and its sheer daring as radio of the very highest order. In The Game Is Not The Same *he explained it thus:*

ALAN McGILVRAY

Radio of the day was not sufficiently advanced technically to rely on direct broadcast from England. Short wave transmissions were occasionally receivable, but they had not at that stage developed procedures to bounce the signal off the ionosphere with any reliability. Moses decided we had to do something ourselves. His *modus operandi* was to establish a commentary team in the ABC studios in Market Street, Sydney, which would recreate what was going on in England.

Their information would be provided by a cable service specially provided from England. The effect would be the same. The commentators would describe the scene as if they were watching with their own eyes. The only thing that would be different was the fact that the eyes had to be on the other side of the world. Those eyes belonged to Eric Sholl, an ABC employee with an eye for detail who worked in the Sydney office.

He was despatched to send back the cables according to an elaborate code. Outside our studio, a team of five or six decoders would put the cables into readable form from which the commentators would operate. The cables covered everything we would need to paint a word picture of what was happening. Sholl would tell us about the weather, the crowd—even the traffic getting to the ground.

He would keep us totally informed as to where every player was on the field. Any time the field changed, he would fire off a new cable, and each over, he would send a cable with a complete run down on every ball—where it pitched, what the batsman did, where the ball went, who fielded ... absolutely everything.

In the studio, every possible step was taken to set up an atmosphere for the commentators. A large photograph of the ground, for instance, was suspended in front of us so we had a mental picture of the scene, and the best chance possible for adding some colour into our broadcast. There were four commentators involved, Vic Richardson, Monty Noble, Hal Hooker and myself.

Richardson and Noble had been to England, so they could identify with each of the grounds. Hooker was a fine Sheffield Shield
player, but never quite made the international arena.

Since Vic and Monty knew the scene best, we left most of
the background descriptions to them. Vic knew where all the
cathedrals were, what the pavilions were like, where the noisy
section of the crowd would congregate. But if we were stuck,
there was always that faithful photograph to fall back on.

We had a scorer and a records man, who could keep track of
events and turn up whatever figures we needed to kick things
along. And there was the all-important sound effects man.

He had a series of recordings which would provide the
applause and crowd noises. We had to make a quick judgment
as to whether a shot was a good one or not, whether a player
would be loudly cheered as he left the field or mildly applauded,
whether the crowd would take umbrage at an umpire's decision.
Accordingly we would signal the sound effects man for wild
cheering, loud applause, booing or gentle clapping, depending
on how we thought it would be.

How closely we judged the scene we could never know. But
after a time the sound effects man was an artist at what he did,
and in all my experience of international cricket I doubt I have
ever known a crowd more animated than that which Australians
knew through the England tour of 1938.

The most basic sound effect of all we provided ourselves. This
was the charismatic crack of leather on willow, the marvellous
ring of bat on ball that has so enraptured cricket followers
through the generations.

This we provided with a pencil. A spanking drive through the
covers, hit with a presumed high back lift and a poultice of
flourish, would require a very firm bang on a round piece of
wood on the table. Defensive taps and more gentle strokes were
handled with appropriately proportional force. This led to occasional difficulty. Sometimes our enthusiasm to describe the shot
meant we would have told the world all about it, suddenly
remembered the pencil, and had the crack of the stroke arriving
somewhat belatedly. Other times the effects man would get in
first with the crowd cheering before the shot came. Co-ordinating
mind, voice and pencil through some long and arduous innings
must have been every bit as hard as coping with Farnes, Verity
and Co, as our batsmen were doing.

Sound effects were not the only area in which our enthusiasm initially made it tough for us. The information we were fed came at the end of each over, covering that over in entirety. We would work our way through the six balls, then look for the new cable and the new over.

At first, we were finding an extraordinary delay between the end of an over as we described it and the next cable.

'Where's the telegram?' we would plead as we thrust ourselves into long and arduous fill-in chatter, sometimes to take up several minutes.

Some simple arithmetic eventually forced on me the realisation that I was whipping through in two minutes an over that the bowler in England was taking four minutes to bowl. Since the cables couldn't come any quicker than the balls were being bowled, we soon learned to take more notice of our stop watch and spread each over to more realistic lengths.

But the mistakes and the rough patches were surprisingly few. As we grew accustomed to this rather revolutionary method of describing a cricket match, we became extremely polished at it. We got faster as time went on, and in the end I think it was every bit as colourful and comprehensive as the real thing became in later years.

The key to everything of course, was the information with which we were supplied and the slick work of those who decoded it. The raw cables, sent at the end of each over, were masterpieces of improvisation.

A typical cable would begin: 'BRIGHTENING FLEET-WOOD HAMMOND FULL FIRSTLY TWO HASSETT SEC-ONDLY FULL FOUR STRAIGHT UNCHANCE BOWLER THIRDLY NO BALL FULL TWO OFFDRIVEN RUN APPEAL HUTTON FOURTHLY FOUR SWEPT BOWLER KEEPER OFFPUSHED.'

The decoders would get hold of that, and the message would come into us in slightly fuller form.

First of all we would establish that the weather was brightening and Fleetwood-Smith was the bowler. 'HAMMOND FULL FIRSTLY TWO HASSETT' would come back 'Hammond batting, first ball pitched up, driven, Hassett fielded, ran two'.

Then the cable continued, 'SECONDLY FULL FOUR

STRAIGHT UNCHANCE BOWLER'. That would be inter-
preted as the second was full length to Hammond, driven straight
but uppishly past the bowler for four. Almost a chance.

So we would work off that information, add a touch of atmosphere, try to imagine the scene, and come up with something
like this:

'In comes Fleetwood-Smith, he moves in to bowl to
Hammond and Hammond comes down the wicket and takes it
on the full and he drives it beautifully past Hassett who moves
around behind the ball and fields brilliantly just before it
reaches the boundary rope, and meantime they've run through
for two.'

The second ball we'd read: 'HAMMOND, FLEETWOOD-
SMITH, FULL TOSS, UPPISH STRAIGHT DRIVE, ALMOST
CHANCE, FOUR.'

We'd get that out something like this: 'Hammond again moves
down the wicket and hits him beautifully past the bowler. My
word, that carried. That was almost in the hands of Fleetwood-
Smith, but it went just past him and although he put a hand out
he didn't get near it and it raced past him for four. But it was
certainly past him round about knee high.'

A fair bit of imagination was called for, although we were
desperately careful not to be so carried away as to significantly
risk the accuracy of the reports.

A cable which read 'HAMMOND SWEPT BARNES FOUR'
might end up, 'Hammond sweeps him. He's really got on to that
one and Barnes is tearing around the boundary to cut it off, but
I don't think he'll get it, and he doesn't, and the ball just beats
him over the boundary rope for four.'

Barnes' race around the boundary, of course, would be greeted
with some enthusiasm by our sound effects man, who would
bring an excited cheer from the crowd, reaching its peak as we
nominated the boundary. He really became quite expert at producing a crowd reaction fitting for each event, and timed to
perfection.

We could operate with quite remarkable efficiency on fairly
skeletal information. We always knew where everybody was in
the field, for instance, so with brief information on the rough
direction on a shot we could assume a likely scenario as far as
the fieldsmen were concerned. And the advantage of having men
like Richardson and Noble involved, men who knew their cricket

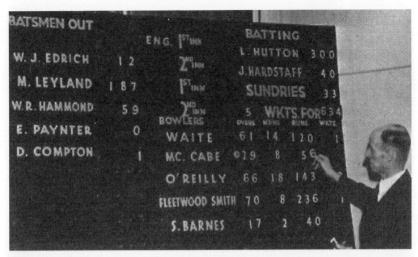

The commentary team for the synthetic Tests had a scoreboard for realism and hardworking production backup.

and their cricketers backwards, was that they could read the game with singular clarity.

Their knowledge of how the Australian players, particularly, thought and performed, their habits and their idiosyncracies, allowed them to gauge reactions and assume trends of play with extraordinary accuracy.

There were, however, times when we were confronted with absolute disaster. Occasionally the flow of cables from the Post Office would be interrupted for one reason or another. When the delays were long we would simply announce a loss of communication and cease operations until they resumed.

But when the loss of contact was brief, or while we thought it would be brief, we tried to tough it out. We might slip in a few balls to mark time. We were always careful in such crises, however, never to advance the score beyond what we knew it to be. Any of these 'fill-in' deliveries would of necessity be insignificant, 'back-to-the-bowler' stuff.

And we filled the gaps with some of the most horrendous discussion. We used to get quite animated. We would be locked in heavy discussion and quite lively argument on subjects that were only imagined.

'He really should be moving forward to those deliveries that are pitched up to him and having a bit of a go,' Vic might offer. 'Well, I don't know about that Vic,' I would reply. 'The bowling's pretty tight and I think the batsmen are quite right in being cautious and taking their time.' The verbal battle would ensue. We would argue the point hammer and tongs, completely oblivious to the fact that neither of us really knew how the batsmen were approaching it, or whether the bowling was good, bad or indifferent. But we became so involved in the broadcasts we almost convinced ourselves we were there. It is quite amazing how the mind and the imagination can take over completely in such circumstances.

A SUMMER HERITAGE

by *Frank Crook*

Frank Crook is an ABC Radio presenter, who worked for many years as a sporting journalist with Sydney newspapers. He was cricket writer for the Sun *in the early 1980s, and toured England with Kim Hughes' side in 1981.*

FRANK CROOK

Those of us who work in the media are forever running into people who believe we hold down the best job in the world.

And they are right, up to a point. We tend to be welcomed where others are forbidden to tread—football dressing rooms, for instance, or a locker room after a title fight, surrounded by bandages, soiled dressings and hard-luck stories, heady with the smell of linament, shoulder to shoulder with our brothers-in-arms, jostling for a position at the front of the pack, hanging on every lacerated syllable from the champ–challenger.

Sometimes, if luck runs our way, we are seated high in a grandstand, binoculars at the ready, watching an Australian thrashing his way through a swimming pool, a gold medal and a world record getting closer with every stroke.

Nobody ever asks us how we feel at the end of a race, yet the adrenalin courses through our veins as well. We are also swept away by the majesty of the moment.

And even when the majesty of the moment begins to fade, we get a spurt on again. That is when we have to riffle through pages of scrawled and scribbled notes and try to make some sense of them.

At the other end of the telephone—or these days the computer terminal—is an editor whose adrenalin is also flowing. There is absolutely nothing like a tight deadline to concentrate the mind.

Watching an event is all very well, but really anyone with the price of a ticket can do that. The real buzz is writing about it later, formulating your thoughts and emotions into a description of what has gone before. That is where the real pleasure lies. And the reason for this is not what the average person suspects.

Traditionally we are expected to swell with pride because we are among the chosen few able to bring our thoughts and views to a large reading and listening public.

I am sure that is all very nice. But we get our kicks mainly because of the very act of reporting. We report, therefore we are. The reader is secondary to the equation.

It all lies in the thrill of being an eye-witness of history, whether it is an Olympic final, a tied Test, a coup in Somalia or a tearful concession from a defeated Prime Minister.

The heart beats faster and the blood pumps and as we leave our seats the word picture begins to form in our minds. It is all part of the fun.

The other charge comes from being close to those whose achievements are part of the business of news. What youngster ever thinks, as he works his way through high school, that one day he will lounge against a fence and chat to Shane Warne about his flipper, or inspect the pitch at Edgbaston with Rodney Marsh, or clap Jeff Fenech on the shoulder and whisper commiserations in his ear.

When we were kids, playing cricket in the street with a dustbin as a wicket, everybody wanted to be Keith Miller. Our great regret in those days was that there were not enough Keith Millers to go around, a view probably shared by the Australian selectors of the day.

But if you missed out on being Miller you could always be Harvey or Morris or Lindwall or Tallon, or Big Bill Johnston or Slammin' Sammy Loxton. We were lucky kids because we grew up in an age of heroes.

And every now and then we would actually meet our heroes. We would cycle through Centennial Park the mile or so to the Sydney Cricket Ground to watch the Australian players practise.

One memorable day Lindsay Hassett, then Australian captain, allowed me to carry his kit into the dressing room. It was the highlight of my young life at the time and still a pleasant memory today.

One day we fielded for Sid Barnes, when that old campaigner, hot on the comeback trail, wanted to swat a few into the outfield. We were, I recall, hunted from the field by a hatchet-faced SCG functionary.

This was the same year the Test selectors refused to choose Barnes, despite a mountain of runs, for 'reasons other than cricket'.

Keith Miller—a brilliant fieldsman

We were convinced it was because Sid had allowed us kids on to the field to fox balls for him.

On another occasion we bowled in the nets to a young Richie Benaud, who was about to make his Test debut against the West Indies. It had rained the previous night and the Australians had cancelled their practice session, but it seems no one had told Richie.

So there we were at the nets—Richie Benaud and a gaggle of kids from Randwick. Rather than waste the afternoon Richie tossed

Keith Miller—always aggressive with the bat

us the ball and we wheeled them down until sunset. The next day we told the kids at school how we took Richie's wicket.

We went to every match we could in those days, arriving for a Test match around eight in the morning to grab a seat along the fence at the bottom of the old Hill in front of the scoreboard. There we'd sit throughout the day, with our sandwiches and bottles of lemonade.

Keith Miller was one of the most enduring and closest of Mac's cricketing friends. Always an electrifying player whether batting, bowling or fielding, he was perhaps the most charismatic player of his era.

Flicking through an old autograph book recently I came across the signature of the young David Sheppard, later to become The Rev David Sheppard, England captain and Bishop of Woolwich in that order.

The good Bishop-to-be had fielded on the fence for much of the afternoon and had obliged the youngsters on the perimeter of the field

*Whimsical Lindsay Hassett, a former Australian captain and sports store
proprietor, who formed a memorable broadcasting partnership with Mac for nearly
20 years. Frank Crook treasures the boyhood memory of carrying Hassett's kit into
the dressing room on one of Frank's many visits to the SCG.*

with his autograph—a Christian act none of us forgot in the interven-
ing years.

But when matches were played outside Sydney, or some child-
hood ailment kept us away from the ground, we turned to our radios
and the voices of cricket—Alan McGilvray, Johnny Moyes, Arthur
Gilligan, Charles Fortune and Victor Richardson. It really was the next
best thing to being there.

Ian Chappell says he knew what every ground in England looked
like when he arrived on his first tour thanks to the descriptive word
pictures painted by that artist of the English language Alan McGilvray.

Norman Tasker, in his eulogy at McGilvray's Memorial Service,
said McGilvray's voice was as much a part of an Australian summer
as the banging of a screen door as a southerly gathered force.

Listening to that voice, on tapes of his bygone broadcasts, all
these images and more filter through the mind . . . the stillness of the
heat of summer, how the SCG pickets shimmered in the
sunlight . . . the hush that fell over the ground as Lindwall marked
out his run for the opening delivery to Hutton.

In the days before television became part of our lives, the voice
of McGilvray was the embodiment of the Summer Game. Every
delivery and every field change was described in detail and described
with understatement and a reverence for the English language.

The voices of cricket, left to right: Johnnie Moyes, Charles Fortune, Arthur
Gilligan and Mac. Fortune, the flamboyant South African, is sporting his
trademark unknotted tie.

Unlike today, when a television call of a Test match sounds more like a Gladiators semi-final, McGilvray and his team provided us with a tone of reassurance. When McGilvray said: 'Australia now five wickets down and a good deal depends on this pair,' it was the cue to inch closer to the radio and concentrate on every ball, like a batsman who had just entered the nineties.

Good manners were always important to McGilvray and his good manners came across the airwaves with every utterance. I like to think that perhaps his good manners may have rubbed off on his young listeners as well as his precise way with words.

It was a much-parodied style among those of my generation. It was considered quite a party trick to do a phantom call of a Test match and capture McGilvray's soft tonal nuances.

As a teenager, I had a hand in writing a sketch for a stage revue based on the McGilvray commentary team, comprising three old fogies called Alec McGillicuddy, Arthur Finnegan and Charles Torture. In the sketch, the cricket ebbed and flowed around them as they discussed the local flora and fauna and poured each other endless cups of tea.

No disrespect was intended and I like to think that McGilvray, a man not without a sense of humour, would have seen the funny side.

That was, of course, years before I actually met the Great Man, who once told me in passing of an absent-minded country cricket committeeman in England who always addressed him as 'Mr Mc-Gillicuddy'. Life imitates art yet again.

Actually, the voice of McGilvray once saved me from a bout of punishment at school.

I had been summoned to the headmaster's office for some misdemeanour or other and was told to expect a dose of the corporal punishment so much in vogue in those days.

With trembling hand I rapped on the headmaster's office door and an impatient voice bid me enter. There was the headmaster, huddled close to his radio as England battled to stave off defeat against Australia.

'Hang on,' said the Head, waving me to a chair, 'I want to get the score.'

The commentary rolled on, like waves on a distant shore until the reverie was broken by Miller—who else but Miller?—grabbing a one-hander at slip and sending the batsman on his way.

'You beauty!' cried the Head. 'We've got them now.'

He then looked me up and down with a curious expression, as though he wasn't quite sure why I was there.

'All right lad,' he said after a long silence, 'on your way then.'

It was really no surprise that the headmaster was whiling away his afternoon listening to McGilvray's description of a Test match. In those days it was the nearest thing we had to a national pastime.

You could walk down any street on a summer afternoon and hear the voice of McGilvray coming from shopfronts and doorways, cutting through the drone of the cicadas.

It all sounded so reasoned and unflappable and delivered with such aplomb that it never occurred to any of us that it was a job of work to McGilvray, merely honest toil, like weighing a bag of potatoes or delivering the milk.

It seemed beyond comprehension that someone actually got paid for a job that entailed watching Test cricket every day and—even better still—getting to tell people about it.

McGilvray's career has been well chronicled over the years, from his landmark simulated broadcasts of the 1930s to his century of Tests. He retired from broadcasting in much the same manner as he had entered it and continued for half a century—without fuss or desire for public acclaim.

We toured England with the side led by Kim Hughes in 1981 and it is on tour that the real McGilvray persona emerges. Away from the broadcasting box McGilvray was indeed a boon companion, who always seemed to have a bottle of Scotch in his room that he was keen to share with anyone who felt like discussing cricket for an hour or two. A couple of years before I had discovered the at first disconcerting McGilvray ritual of disposing of the cork the instant a bottle was broached. It meant no one left the room alive until the bottle was empty.

That thin line between life and death was always a blurry one the morning after a McGilvray soiree. We would troop to our places in the press box, halt of limb and avoiding the sunlight and there was McGilvray, immaculate as ever, club tie knotted just so and blue blazer free of lint.

His drinking companions of the night before looked as though they'd slept in their clothes, as indeed some of them had.

As we tried to untangle our fingers from typewriter keys and jumped at the slightest sound, McGilvray's commentary began, precise and controlled, moving inexorably through over after over, rather like Bradman building an innings, solid, mistake-free with flashes of brilliance.

Talk to McGilvray at the end of a day's play and his deep knowledge of the game came into full flower. He had the ability to dissect a session with the dexterity of a micro-surgeon. He pinpointed where captains went wrong in areas like field placement, bowling changes and identifying batsmen's weaknesses.

Often you wished he would pull the skipper aside and impart some of the McGilvray wisdom on the subject of tactics, gleaned from decades of watching and listening.

But that was never the McGilvray way of doing things. If they didn't ask, he wouldn't offer. There were certainly times though, when a few words of McGilvray advice may well have turned that 1981 series, particularly when we were watching Botham butcher our attack—Lillee, Alderman and Lawson included—at Headingley. All we could do was turn our eyes to the sky and cry: 'Why doesn't someone do something?' I'm sure McGilvray would have had a plan.

In a way it was a pity that the final years of McGilvray's career in the broadcasting box coincided with both Australia's decline in the Test arena and the rise of limited-overs cricket.

He saw little good in the shortened version of the game, nor did he admire the departure from the traditional uniforms. But he tended to keep his opinions to himself.

Yet he was no hidebound traditionalist like many of his generation. He believed, for instance, that there was merit in playing first-class matches limited only to 100 overs in the first innings.

He held up as an example of this the Melbourne Centenary Test, which became a gripping encounter after each side had posted a moderate first innings total.

When he retired from broadcasting, McGilvray told friends he had no plans to attend matches as a spectator. 'I've seen enough to last me all my life,' he said at the time.

But the lure of cricket is a strong one and before long McGilvray was back where he belonged, either quietly watching the game from a seat in the Members Stand or greeting old acquaintances in his favourite spot in the bar of the MA Noble Stand, named after his old mentor Alf Noble who, one day long ago, plotted with a young McGilvray the downfall of the mighty Bradman in a Shield game.

The memories would have flooded back as he looked around the

A full house at the SCG in the early 1930s. In clear view are the hill and the old scoreboard on the right and the Paddington hill on the left.

ground ... of Verity and Tate and Gubby Allen, of Grimmett and O'Reilly, of good manners and good sportsmanship and the sounds of a summer day.

Just as the memories flood back for a boy who avoided the cane because a Test match was being played and McGilvray was on the air.

As a cricket tactician, Alan McGilvray's mind was always working and as Frank Crook relates, there were many occasions when it seemed a captain in trouble might well benefit from the wisdom available in the commentary box.

McGilvray had a remarkable empathy with the captains he watched operate in the field. He would never impose his views, but he was always available to give them if asked. On one famous occasion, the 1981 Australian captain Kim Hughes tapped into the McGilvray experience, and was given what turned out to be very sound advice. To his great cost, Hughes chose to ignore it.

The following extract tells the tale, from Captains Of The Game.

ALAN McGILVRAY

At his best Hughes was a beautiful batsman with a wide array of strokes, aggressive footwork and considerable power. But his best seemed to become buried in the difficulties of his captaincy. He played like a sea captain going down with his ship. He seemed totally dominated by the need to assert himself, a sort of feigned confidence that brought him undone time after time.

Hughes became the classic batsman for 30 or 40 runs who rarely went on with the job. Centuries that had seemed there for the taking were sacrificed on the altar of unthinking aggression. Hughes assumed he could hammer everything, no matter how good the bowler, how bad the pitch or how tenuous the Australian position. He played some marvellous innings nontheless. The awesome power of his century at Lord's in the English centenary Test was pure majesty. But I always had the feeling he could have done that over and over, had he been more the mature batsman, and less the angry young man.

His captaincy, as well as his batting, was badly undermined by his naked aggression. I always considered there was a very fine line for Hughes between total attack and desperate defence. Sometimes it seemed almost as if he had shut his eyes, swung the bat and hoped. It was hardly the responsible, fighting example for a captain to put before his troops and there developed in the Australian side a sort of brittle unpredictability. It made the game something of a lottery.

Tactically, Hughes suffered badly by the tour of England in 1981. Having won the first Test, he was ideally placed to win both the third and the fourth Tests, which would have given Australia a 3–0 series lead. He managed to lose them both.

The tour represented Hughes' first really big test. It was his first experience in charge of the post-WSC Test side which meant he had forces like Marsh and Lillee under his command. He began with enormous drive and enthusiasm. In the first Test at Nottingham, Australia needed only 132 in the second innings to win, but were making heavy weather of it at 5–122 before they eventually won the day. Once he was out we invited Hughes to join us in the commentary box, which he gladly did. As the tension grew, his contribution to the commentary became increasingly animated.

He forgot all about telling the people at home anything. He yelled encouragement to the batsmen, and cheered and groaned with every ball. For the professional commentators there with him, it was a quite hilarious scene, but a very poignant one as well: a young man, captain of his country, totally embroiled in his team and their welfare. Such enthusiasm deserved a much better reward than was eventually to befall Hughes in the later Tests of that tour.

By Headingley and the third Test, with a win and a draw behind him, it seemed it was all systems go for Hughes. But there was always a question about the Leeds pitch, and he knew it. He asked me to go to the ground with him early on the morning of the game, and when he sought my opinion on how the wicket might play, I had one simple word of advice for him.

'Whatever you do, Kim,' I said, 'don't bat last.' In the event, Australia led by 227 on the first innings, but Hughes ignored my entreaties and asked England to follow-on. There followed an assault by Ian Botham which gave him 149 not out, and left Australia with a 130-run target in the last innings of the match. They were all out for 111, giving England one of the more remarkable victories of Test match history and, I am pained to say, making Kim Hughes look very silly indeed.

The fourth Test went sour as well, and Hughes returned to Australia beaten and chastened. His captaincy was troubled from that point on. Greg Chappell resumed the captaincy, handed it back to Hughes, then resumed it again before Hughes was finally made captain in his own right upon Chappell's retirement. Success was hard to come by, and drama never far away. Eventually it all became too much.

On the final day's play of the second Test against West Indies in 1984–85, Hughes approached the team vice-captain, Allan Border, before play and told him he intended to resign the captaincy that afternoon. Border cautioned him to reconsider but Hughes had taken the decision, and as he read his resignation statement to the world at the after-match press conference, he broke down and was unable to continue. It was a very sad exit.

I felt for Kim Hughes. He was a man with a lot of talent and an engaging personality, and I liked him. He might even have been an adequate captain had he been allowed to grow into the role as good captains must. But he was thrown in at one of Australian cricket's most turbulent periods, and in circumstances which simply gave him no chance. He was, perhaps, the most spectacular victim of the World Series Cricket revolution.

Kim Hughes pulling viciously during his powerful century at Lord's, Centenary Test, 1980. Here he succeeded but often his single-minded aggression led to his demise.

AN HONORARY POM

by David Frith

David Frith is an Australian who has lived and worked in England for many years, establishing himself as one of its leading cricket authorities. He was for many years editor of the respected cricket magazine Wisden Cricket Monthly.

DAVID FRITH

Even now, so many years after his final cricket broadcast in England, there are people who still regard Alan McGilvray as the best commentator of all. They liked his 'better-class' Australian accent and they liked his objectivity. His knowledge and feel for the game stood out clearly, and even the most biased 'Pom' would never have accused 'Mac' of siding with 'his' team, the Australian visitors.

Now this is quite remarkable when the mass worship of the local cricket commentators, John Arlott and Brian Johnston, is taken into account. Years after their deaths, their voices are missed grievously by the generations who literally grew up listening to them: the warm Hampshire baritone of the poetic Arlott and the lovable nonsense dispensed by 'Johnners', who seems to have been regarded as almost everybody's favourite uncle.

'McGillers', as Johnston named him, stood on his own pedestal in the UK, like Richie Benaud on television, Rolf Harris everywhere, and Clive James in between. And that's a rare achievement, for to be quite blunt about it, Australia's stocks in Britain have slipped in recent years. It's all about image and politics—and the fact that Englishmen really have to probe deeply into memory to recall when their Test team last dominated Australia.

Alan McGilvray's popularity sprang, of course, from his impeccable manners and old-world standards. Those in the know realised that he had played Sheffield Shield cricket pre-war, and had even schemed Bradman out, and that his association with

England went back to 1948. And there is no more auspicious association than being linked with Don Bradman's triumphant final tour of the Old Country.

McGilvray did 10 ABC cricket tours of England all told, including all of the Ashes series between 1961 and 1985, and he therefore became a kind of fixture with each of those Australian tours. He never had occasion to get upset in England while on duty, as he did in the Caribbean, because crowds never got out of hand; any animosity generated by England v Australia Test matches tends to be low-key, almost 'in the family'.

But it would be a pretence to claim that all was well at all times in the BBC commentary box, for there were tensions, mainly between McGilvray and Arlott. Both were good friends, and, privately, I heard them both explaining the problem from their own viewpoint. Alan, justifiably, disliked having the day's roster altered during the first session of play. Like a batsman preparing himself, he needed to know what number he would be batting. There was also the crucial matter of the links to Australia. He had a theory that John, for all his great stature as a cricket commentator, never threw off an insecurity about his technical knowledge of the game. He therefore felt more comfortable following someone like Johnston, whose grasp of cricket's theory and practice left much to be desired. He was the Entertainer, the Cheerer-Up. But Arlott knew that at the end of Johnners' 20 minutes, the cognoscenti were longing to know what really was going on out in the middle. Notwithstanding the between-overs expert summariser, Alan McGilvray was always on top of the game and inside the key players' heads.

Trevor Bailey, the dour England allrounder of the 1950s and longtime BBC cricket comments man, makes no bones about it: 'McGilvray had no time for Arlott, and vice versa. McGilvray was a very good commentator *and* a very good cricketer, and it jolted. There was a clash of personalities.'

It was a credit to both of them, and their producer, that the general public never detected even a glimmer of discord in the box, and it warmed my heart, knowing of the rivalry as I did, to find Alan McGilvray sitting comfortably in one of John Arlott's armchairs when I called into his Hampshire home on one of countless visits.

There is one reservation. This little bit of socialising may well have been *before* the occasion when Mac sat down for his next spell of commentary only to discover that Arlott, who had just vacated the box, had been taking shallots (onions), which, with a touch of claret,

John Arlott at the microphone for the BBC. Arlott was Mac's main rival for the title of best ever cricket broadcaster. Throughout their long association, the pair had at best a grudging respect for each other and a relationship kept at arm's length.

had left an overpowering set of aromas in the air. McGilvray insisted on a fresh microphone!

Rex Alston, who broadcast with Alan during his first tour of England, in 1948, described him as a 'lovely broadcaster', but the man who probably spent most time with him over his BBC years was Brian Johnston, and he probably envied Mac, in the best possible

On Mac's 1948 tour of England as a guest commentator for the BBC, Rex Alston and John Arlott made up the rest of the team. Alston, a former school teacher, was noted for his flowery language and the players referred to him as 'Rex Balston'.

way. He called him the 'whispering commentator' because of his intimate style of talking: softly into a lip microphone, so that others in the box could barely hear him. Johnston marvelled at his use of binoculars, which he himself found impossible to handle while perched over a mike—perhaps a legacy of his wartime experiences in tanks. He noted, too, that McGilvray shunned flowery language. There was, after all, enough of that flowing from the mouths of others.

Wickedly, though, Brian Johnston set up Alan McGilvray whenever he could, and Alan, being a serious chap, managed to survive, with a shrug and a diffident smile. There was the time he was invited to have his fill of chocolate cake (symbol of *Test Match Special* on the BBC). Mouth loaded, he was then asked for his views on something or other. Never one to shirk his professional obligations, Alan made a gallant attempt at response, but cake crumbs exploded everywhere and that wonderful voice struggled hopelessly to get past the congested larynx and tongue.

Another time, he was taking a nap at the back of the box when Johnners swung round and referred a question to him, telling listeners that Alan McGilvray was sure to have something interesting to say on this particular matter. The confusion was twofold, Johnston hurriedly pretending that Mac was not, after all, available, and Mac suddenly awakening. Don Mosey, hysterical with laughter, fled the box, while Brian Johnston was prostrate with mirth. For quite some time all that the BBC's eager listeners could pick up was a kind of wheezing sniggering. Well might Alan McGilvray have reflected on his prewar synthetic cricket broadcasts, with all their disciplines and their malfunctions.

Without quite cracking the aristocratic world as Jack Fingleton and Arthur Mailey did on their tours of England (it gave them huge satisfaction to hobnob with the lords and the showbiz set when they

Brian Johnston, better known as 'Johnners', was very popular in both England and Australia. A decorated war hero, he followed the unusual path of starting his cricket broadcasting with the BBC on television and finishing on radio.

reflected on their humble origins), Alan McGilvray enjoyed his visits, though he moved around unostentatiously. It was only with a sense of duty that he attended the launch of his book, *The Game Is Not The Same*, after the last Test of the unhappy (for Australians) 1985 tour. Some of us stood around with Mac, talking in desultory fashion, and sinking a glass or two. It was very companionable. Then the subject turned to Don Bradman, and Mac's eyes lit up. For the next few minutes we were out there on the pitch with them in the 1930s, and our narrator gave a rounded picture of the Greatest Batsman, reinforcing the impression of his supremacy, but dropping in an occasional wart. It was living history.

Alan cared deeply about Australia's image, and during the 1977 tour of England he was distressed by the sloppy dress standards of many of the Australian players. I think he felt they were letting their country down, projecting a bad impression. At the hotels, some of the cricketers would come down to breakfast in T-shirts and shorts, and Alan would scowl and mumble to himself. I'm sure he was conjuring up visions of some of the Australian players from the 1930s, men of style and grace and dash and courtesy, like Alan Kippax and Bert Oldfield, even Vic Richardson, grandfather of the Chappell brothers, one of whom was leading the Australian Test team on this very tour while his elder brother was a key figure in Kerry Packer's breakaway movement. It was a hard time for traditionalists.

Eventually, Alan McGilvray decided he had had enough. At one of the receptions, he stood by the door. As the Australian cricketers arrived, he would give them an almost regimental inspection, from top to toe, and pass comment where he felt it was deserved.

One particular young player was regarded in some circles as a likely Australian captain of the future. So when he turned up in casual clothes, with no necktie at his collar, Mac upbraided him. He suggested that as a possible future Test skipper he ought to have known better than to turn up at such a function improperly dressed. To the young man's credit, he politely pointed out that he was not yet captain, and in all probability would never become captain, and it *was* a warm evening, and so on. Mac flushed a little. He had done what he saw as his duty.

One of the things I liked about him was his freedom of movement among players new and old, irrespective of their nationality. When he talked with Len Hutton and Colin Cowdrey, Jim Laker and Godfrey Evans, he was talking to men who were truly friends. This had much to do with the Ashes tradition, stemming from the closeness of

England's great post-war wicketkeeper Godfrey Evans, famous for his mutton-chop whiskers, became notable in later years as Ladbroke's cricket adviser for the betting shops. He was a true friend of Mac's. Patrick Eagar

Australia and England in the old days, and Alan, just like RG Menzies and many another, myself included, saw the drifting apart of these countries year by year as a source of anguish.

In his own book, he conveys his affection for the 'green fields of England', and makes it clear why he found his many tours there no hardship at all: 'The grandeur of English cricket, of course, goes a lot deeper than the wonderful atmosphere of its grounds and the dignity of its traditions. England down the years has supplied in greater numbers than any other nation the most graceful and the most articulate players. There is a certain style to their play, an almost hereditary leaning towards the artistic.'

Daily on tour, he showed that it was possible to be proudly Australian and yet appreciative of other places and people. This dignity in his make-up is what persuaded the English cricket fraternity to trust him and like him. And it was all genuine.

It could easily have been otherwise. Alan McGilvray must have wondered if the 1948 tour would be not only his first visit to England but his last, for the local commentators gave him an icy reception. He has himself described the daunting experience of near-rejection when he first sat in an English commentary box. It was at Hove, when the Australians played Sussex, and Rex Alston, ever the schoolmaster, issued what Alan could only feel was a warning: None of that colonial stuff here, old chap. He was withdrawn prematurely, and his blood must have run cold when he heard John Arlott's voice down the line, saying that McGilvray couldn't possibly be allowed to broadcast.

It makes incredible reading now, for the Australian later rose to become an institution in England as well as in his homeland. Whether, as he claimed, English commentary soon switched to the more Australian 'factual' style is, I believe, somewhat open to question. The score is still not given all that often—certainly not three times per over, as Mac deemed essential—and the 'terribly lyrical' style preferred by English commentators still tempts them—'the birds, the clouds, dress trends'—even if the current crop have nothing like the imagination and constructive powers of an Arlott. It was a relief to establish that that unhappy start to their acquaintance—Arlott and McGilvray—was eventually put right. It was only fitting, for they remain two of the most impressive men, in their separate ways, that I have ever been privileged to know.

The opinion of perhaps the biggest heavyweight of all, EW Swanton, probably covers England's view of Alan McGilvray most accurately. 'His work at the microphone,' Jim wrote, 'has had for me other admirable qualities beyond his basic style, and the chief of these is a complete objectivity and absence of bias. Were it not for the Australian inflexion, one could not tell where his personal sympathies lay.

'His critical judgments have been not only sound but eminently fair and consistently generous.'

Jim Swanton, in keeping with all senior observers, was quick to recognise Mac's moral rectitude too: 'He is the enemy, thank goodness, of all that cheapens the game or threatens the values which were taken for granted in every generation before Packerism cast its ugly shadow on it. In Australia the last eight years [i.e. since 1977] his cricket generation has been fighting a particularly tough uphill battle.'

You can see here more clearly than ever what it was that endeared McGilvray to the English. Chauvinism breeds counter-chauvinism, and jingoism breeds like too. There was none of this about him, and his hosts consequently never felt threatened.

And it must have been comparatively easy for him to maintain this even stance, for he not only cherished cricket and all that it stood for, but he loved Australia and adored England. O, happy man.

The problem finally became one of disillusionment. The game sure has changed. It certainly is 'not the same'. And both these nations have changed, perhaps in keeping with the aspirations of the young, but not always in line with the requirements of the McGilvray generation.

We mourn the departure of favourite players as retirement swallows them up, and the same applies to the commentators. When Alan McGilvray died in July 1996, at the age of 86, the tributes in the British papers were heartfelt. He had been missed already for the 11 years since he last breathed his intimate descriptions into a BBC microphone. No-one, it seems, has been able to match the urgency he brought to a quick single: would the batsman beat the throw? I always believed he was, in spirit, out there himself, swooping on the ball and throwing on the turn, Bertie Oldfield's gloves waiting eagerly by the bails.

If proof were needed that he was accepted by England as one of her own (in spite of the surname!), then consider the MBE awarded to him by the British Government in 1974. In that appointment, old-fashioned though it now seems, Alan McGilvray saw his name placed alongside others who were similarly honoured, such as Lindsay Hassett, Keith Miller, Ian Johnson, Neil Harvey, Ray Lindwall, Arthur Morris, and Richie Benaud. Every one of them has been regarded as a favourite in London town and the provinces. In that respect they have done much more for Australia than just make runs and take wickets . . . and describe Test matches over the radio-waves.

As David Frith has recounted, Alan McGilvray's introduction to broad-casting in England was by no means universally welcomed. His style was very different from that in vogue in England at the time, and initially it was resented. In later years McGilvray made no secret of the fact that his early experiences of the 1948 tour of England hurt him.

Ultimately, of course, it made his universal acceptance in England as a commentator of unique ability that much more remarkable. In the end, after ten tours with Australian sides, he had built such a following that the crowd at The Oval for his final Test gave him a standing ovation as a gesture of farewell.

In the following extract from The Game Is Not The Same, *McGilvray recalls the difficulty of his early encounter with cricket commentary in England, and the legendary John Arlott . . .*

ALAN McGILVRAY

My introduction to broadcasting cricket in England was at Hove, where the Australians were engaged in an early tour match against Sussex. I was very much bound up in the general high spirits that prevailed as I made my way up to the box and was greeted by Rex Alston, a well-known broadcaster and writer on cricket. The deal was that I would describe the last twenty minutes before lunch, then give a summary for Australia. Outside of that, I was available to the BBC team to use as they saw fit.

When my time came to broadcast, Alston was very careful to remind me that I was broadcasting to Britain, through the BBC, as well. Whether it was his meaning or not, I took his reminder as something of a warning. None of that colonial stuff here, old chap. This is England! I began my commentary, ready for a twenty-minute stint.

At the end of just one over Alston chipped in, thanked me, explained to everybody that I was the Australian broadcaster over for the tour, and commandeered the microphone. I sat waiting for an invitation to resume. None came. Then I heard the voice of John Arlott, whom at that stage I had not met, coming over the headphones from a ground in the north of England. He left little doubt as to what he thought of Mc-Gilvray's first broadcast in England.

'Rex, what on earth have you got there?' was the substance

of his inquiry. 'You can't possibly let him broadcast.'

At that stage I admit to being somewhat confused and disillusioned about my role as a cricket commentator in England. Oh well, I thought, at least I can spend some time over here checking out shoe factories and buying some equipment for my father's business back home.

The substance of Alston's reluctance and Arlott's thumbs down was, as it turned out, a matter of style. At that time English commentators and Australian commentators did things very differently.

The English practice was to be terribly lyrical. They would talk about the birds, and the clouds and all manner of things. Their commentaries were rich with colour and atmosphere, but it didn't seem to matter if they missed a ball or two while they were discussing dress trends for the gentry in the Long Room.

My style was rather more direct. I would describe the ball, analyse every ball, give the score at least three times an over and often more, generally cover everything that happened. The BBC team saw that as being fairly dull. Certainly they weren't used to it.

By the end of that 1948 tour, though, my style, as practised by all Australian commentators since the very start of radio in Australia, had taken a considerable hold in Britain. We were getting an enormous amount of letters which indicated to the BBC that this new approach, which described every ball, was very popular. Others from Australia, of course, have done the same, but it is gratifying now to all Australian broadcasters who have been to England to see the way English commentary has changed. Strictly speaking, they now do it our way—the way Arlott and Co had found so distasteful that very first day at Hove.

Arlott was one of the first to recognise the value of a direct, ball to ball approach, and by the end of the tour was telling me that my style had found quite an appeal. I recounted his words that I had heard on the earphones at the start of the tour. Taken aback as he was, he smiled as if to say, 'We all make mistakes'.

One of the more eloquent supporters of our particular Australian method was the great Australian Prime Minister Sir Robert Menzies, whose abiding love of cricket went back to the days before Word War I when Barnes and Foster were tearing through Australia's batting. Those were the days of Trumper and Ransford, of Bardsley and Armstrong, of Hobbs and Woolley.

Sir Robert's boyhood love of the game, born in the midst of such superlative performers, never left him. During his record term as Australian Prime Minister, first in the early days of World War II and again from 1949 until he retired in 1966, Sir Robert won a reputation for his unswerving devotion to all things British. But when it came to listening to the cricket, he was very Australian.

'What we all like about you,' he once told me, during an interview at Lord's on the occasion of the 200th Test between England and Australia, 'is that instead of regaling us on the state of the sky, or the condition of the flowers, or the seagulls on the ground or whatever, you always tell us the state of play. Who hit that ball, where it went, what runs resulted, if any, and what the state of the game is. And for that, sir, I thank you most profoundly.'

Sir Robert fancied himself as something of a coach as far as my broadcasting was concerned. As Australia's most brilliant orator, he made a study of words and their usage.

'The pause, Alan,' he used to tell me, 'can be almost as eloquent as any word. Use the pause. Slow down.'

I often tried to make the point with him that the pause he used so skilfully in the nation's forums when people hung on every word, was more difficult to employ when a ball had flown like a rocket to slips, a man had dived to take it, and a crowd was roaring itself hoarse in instant response.

I think deep down Sir Robert would have liked to have been a cricket commentator. Certainly he was a great champion for cricket. And, thankfully, he was a heartfelt supporter of the type of broadcasting I employed, and which at first found such little favour with my English contemporaries.

John Arlott, I must concede, did not endear himself to me on that first tour. I considered him fairly high-handed. But as the years have rolled on my respect for him has developed enormously, and these days we are good friends. He was not the most knowledgeable of cricket broadcasters, technically, but he had a unique command of the English language, and the way he has used it around England's cricket fields has given him a singular place in cricket folklore.

He could make a rainy day sound interesting. His colourful turn of phrase, his creative word pictures, could not be matched by any other commentator. You could close your eyes and listen to Arlott's commentaries and see everything as if you were sitting on the mid-on boundary.

His limited background in cricket occasionally came through, particularly early on. I remember Ray Lindwall taking him to task one day in 1948 because he had described Lindwall's deliveries as 'turning from the leg'. Lindwall was moved to explain to Arlott that he didn't turn the ball. He swung it in the air, perhaps cut it off the pitch, but he didn't turn it. He didn't want people back home to think he was turning it. That could mean he was bowling spinners, and I think Ray saw that as some sort of affront to his athleticism.

'Just a matter of expression, dear boy,' Arlott countered. 'Just a matter of expression.'

Arlott is a fantastic person. He won an enormous following as an expert on food and wine with *The Guardian* newspaper in London. He loved his wine and had literally thousands of bottles in his home in Sussex. He would always have a bottle with him at the cricket and, by the time he had dined at night, it was nothing for him to have downed seven bottles in an average day. He had a rule that he would not broadcast after lunch, a concession he made to his love of red wine.

I often wondered how Arlott would have handled the synthetic broadcasts of 1938. Ten years later, of course, communications had improved to the extent that direct broadcasts to Australia from London were quite acceptable, and the days of the synthetics had gone. But Arlott would have been marvellous in that exercise. Regrettably, we didn't see much of John Arlott in Australia. His distaste for flying and travel kept him pretty much at home. He received a standing ovation from the crowd and the players when he finished his final broadcast at the Lord's Centenary Test against Australia in 1980. I joined that ovation, heartily and without reservation, for he had been a truly great cricket commentator.

AN AUSSIE PAL
by David Frith

Denis Compton and Fred Trueman were great England players of their era with whom Alan McGilvray had a particular rapport. He regarded both of them not just as pre-eminent cricketers among England players down the years, but as men who added a great lustre to the game by the attitudes they adopted in all their associations with it. David Frith spoke to each of them about the loss of an 'Aussie mate'.

DAVID FRITH

I knew that Denis Compton and Fred Trueman were special friends, so when Alan McGilvray died I rang them both, and knew immediately that they were deeply saddened by his passing, and had had huge respect for him.

He was always what might be termed a 'player's man', which is not surprising in one who played first-grade cricket and captained New South Wales, mixing with the best of the cream-flannelled breed. So it seems natural that he should have demonstrated sincere concern for Compton when he was in his 'horror stretch' during England's 1950–51 tour of Australia.

'It was awful, that bad trot,' Denis, now 78, recalled. He made 53 runs in four Tests at an average of 7.57, and though he hit the winning runs in England's long-awaited victory in the final Test, at Melbourne, the wretched sequence remained a nightmare to him. And yet he remembers that comfort came most memorably from someone who, he thought, belonged to his opponents' camp.

'Don't worry,' Mac told me. 'All players have a bad trot like this at some stage.' Those words meant a lot to Denis Compton, who only two years previously had been a hero of the first order by scoring 184 against Bradman's Australians in the Nottingham Test and 145 not out at Manchester (after Lindwall had split his brow with a bouncer early in the innings).

'Mind you, I didn't do so badly on the first tour of Australia, in

Denis Compton was a special friend. Patrick Eagar

1946–47,' Compton reflected. 'Alan came into the dressing-room at Adelaide when I got those hundreds in each innings. I thought that was a very nice gesture.'

It turned out to be quite an all-our-yesterdays session when I spoke with England's Brylcreem hero of yesteryear, for he had just had a phone call from his great mate Keith Miller, over in Sydney. And now I was asking him about Alan McGilvray. Were they truly that friendly?

'Oh, my word, yes. He was a great pal of mine. We used to have a few drinks from time to time. He enjoyed that! He loved the game of cricket.' There was that brotherhood feeling, almost unique to cricket.

Fred Trueman shared many great moments with Mac in the BBC commentary box.
Patrick Eagar

'He was a great pal of Miller's,' Denis continued, 'so he was therefore a great pal of mine!'

And as a broadcaster? 'The best in the business. The *best.*'

Later I checked out what McGilvray thought of Compton, and was not the least surprised to read: 'If I had to choose a solitary Englishman as the epitome of all that is fine in English cricket it would certainly be that prince of batsmen, Denis Compton. He was the ultimate entertainer, a player of extraordinary ability who complemented his talents with an ebullient nature and a showman's flair. He was film star quality, and England loved him.'

So, I think, did Australia.

Compton would never again be able to shake hands with

McGilvray, and his parting words were touching and disturbing: 'We were all very good pals in those days. It's not like that so much today.'

So how was the feeling up North? I rang Freddie Trueman, whose hair is still long and appears to be as black as in his halcyon days in the 1950s, when he was rampaging with the new ball for Yorkshire and England.

'Alan? Oo, aye, a great pal, had 'im out to my home when he were over 'ere. *Great* pal.'

Fred was still overcome by the recent passing of Ray Lindwall, and for both of us it was close to being a bit much to bear, all this losing of old friends whom we admired so greatly.

' 'E used to talk about the 1930s. I used to love that. Don Bradman, Ponsford, Harold Larwood . . . and Sid Barnes. 'E was very fond of Barnes.'

Trueman racked his brain, summoning up a picture of the Australian commentator with whom he had passed so many hours in the BBC box. Naturally, he remembered the cholocate-cake set-up, and roars of laughter came down the line. 'Johnners did 'im! Oo, 'e did 'im rotten! Poor old Alan!'

He even reckons that an inadvertent swearword came out of the disciplined McGilvray lips once, though it was so swift and so unlikely that nobody else—certainly no listeners—seemed to notice. Fred almost seemed to regret that it had gone unnoticed.

Oddly, it is other embarrassments that Fred Trueman remembers: ' 'E was going to interview Frank Tyson during the '54–55 Test series in Australia, and Frank didn't show! Alan was a bit, how shall I say, miffed about that.'

And he remembered with pride the time that it rained, and they stayed on the air, and none of the others was around, so FS Trueman and AD McGilvray talked cricket and cricketers to a spellbound listening audience of millions for an hour and 40 minutes. One hundred minutes! Why, Fred could have bowled out an entire Middlesex XI in that time.

'He rated me the best out of all England's fast bowlers, you know.'

I was about to say, 'What, even above Larwood?' But I didn't want to spoil this chat with my old mate. So what sort of a chap did he really find Alan McGilvray to be?

'Serious. He were a quiet sort of commentator. Serious.'

He then thought of something Mac had told him once, about the time he felt unwanted. The reason he felt unwanted was that thousands had come to see Bradman bat in a Shield match at Sydney, and McGilvray had plotted his downfall. Aided by his own mentor, MA Noble, he had urged Bob Hynes to dip one of his fastish left-arm deliveries into the great batsman's pads in the hope that leg slip would get a catch. It worked. Ray Little held the catch. The Don had made a rare duck. And the crowd who had paid their two-bobs in the near-certainty of buying a close-up view of a Bradman hundred or two felt cheated. So Mac, for a few moments at any rate, felt rather abashed, a bit of a party-pooper.

And now he was gone, and two English cricket giants were among the mourners.

'I'll tell you this, David,' said Fred Trueman, 'first thing I've always done when I arrive in Adelaide is to ring Sir Donald. And the first thing I do when I'm in Brisbane is ring Ray Lindwall. And when I'm in Sydney, first person I ring is Alan McGilvray.'

If Fred ever makes it back to Australia, he'll be looking at the telephone with an indescribable sadness.

Fred Trueman's mention of McGilvray's plot, as NSW captain, to dismiss Don Bradman in a Sydney Sheffield Shield match recalls the sharpness of the McGilvray cricket brain, and the help he had in his early years from the great Australian captain of the early 20th century, MA Noble.

The extract from The Game Is Not The Same *begins with a conversation with Bradman after South Australia had beaten New South Wales at the Adelaide Oval. Bradman is looking to the return game in Sydney with some relish.*

ALAN McGILVRAY

'Mac,' he said, with that same determined look in his eye. 'When I get to the Sydney Cricket Ground I'm going to score more runs than I have in any match this season.'

Well, I was well aware he had scored 300-plus in a game earlier that year, and his promise embodied some fairly uncomfortable prospects for us. 'I came up to congratulate you for winning this game,' I retorted, 'but I'll say this. If you're going to score 300 runs on the SCG, you'll be doing a lot of running.'

The exchange certainly inspired in me a new spur for the return game, which I brought up in conversation with Monty Noble. A plan was hatched. Since Bradman's form that season included scores of 117, 233 and 357, we knew it had to be a pretty good plan, to say the least.

Analysing the strengths and weaknesses of cricketers is a captain's job. There is always something to be attacked, some little flaw that offers a glimmer of hope even with the most accomplished players. In Bradman's case, finding a weakness was like finding the lost city of Atlantis. I doubt one really existed.

As Noble and I tried to work out what we might attack, all we could do was analyse his *modus operandi*, and hope that we could in some way take advantage of a pattern.

The best we could come up with was a feeling that Bradman was an uncertain starter. Uncertain, at least, when compared with the majesty of his batting in full flourish. I believed he always liked to get off the mark with a shot around square leg, or slightly behind it, so we reasoned we would feed that shot and try to tighten it a touch for him. But we knew we had to get him before he was ten, or we were gone.

The NSW team of that year had a fairly useful inswing bowler in Bob Hynes. He was the mainspring of our plan. We put a man at fine leg slip, and I parked myself virtually on Bradman's bat, just a yard or so away at short square leg. I knew I had no hope of catching him there, but our object was to force him to play the shot a little more finely than he normally would, and hope that the ball would do enough to give us a chance of a catch at leg slip. In the event, Hynes' first ball was a screamer, which ripped through the Bradman defence that had so thwarted the world's bowlers and caught him on the pads, dead in front.

Up went the appeal. 'Not out,' came the response. Hynes was distraught. 'Mac, he was out!' he pleaded as he came back for the next delivery. Inclined as I was to offer enthusiastic agreement, I could do little else but try to keep his mind on the job. 'Remember what we planned,' I said. 'Forget the last ball, work on the next.'

Down Hynes came again. Bradman shaped to flick him away as we had thought, the ball kicked on him and flew to the fine leg slip, and the mighty man was gone. It was an eerie feeling. You can make a thousand plans on the cricket field and have none of them work. And here we had Bradman for nought, according to a scenario almost identical to that worked out in Monty Noble's office.

'Well, we can dream about that 300,' I said to Bradman as he headed for the pavilion. It was a fairly cheeky thing to say, and it did me no great credit. The eyes burned back at me. At the right moment those Bradman eyes carried as much power as any of his flourishing cover drives.

Not everybody shared our team's joy at Bradman's dismissal. As I left the field I was accosted by a mountain of a man who grabbed me by the shoulders and hoisted me off the ground as though I were a bag of chaff.

'I came 350 miles to see this man bat,' he complained. 'And he's out for a duck. I'll curse you lot with every turn of the wheel on the way home.'

I could offer little more comfort to him than a feeble 'sorry', and headed for the safety of the dressing room as fast as I could get there.

I felt compelled to go to Bradman and ease my conscience over what I had said to him as he left the field.

'I'm not sorry for getting you out,' I began. 'But I am sorry for what I said out there. It was not very gentlemanly, and uncalled for.' I meant it, and I'm sure Bradman knew I meant it. That little smile that says 'You're in trouble, sonny,' creased his face. 'There's always a second innings, you know,' came his retort. I never had any doubt that Bradman would have scored a mountain of runs in the second innings. He believed NSW people considered him washed up, a rather curious judgment when you look at his record over the next twelve years, and he had a passionate desire to succeed spectacularly on the SCG to make his point.

Unfortunately, King George V died that day, the match was abandoned, and we escaped his retribution.

CARIBBEAN CHAOS

by Tony Cozier

Tony Cozier has been a leading commentator and cricket writer in the West Indies since the 1960s, and produces in Barbados the Caribbean's leading cricket magazine. He has been a regular visitor to Australia with West Indies sides over nearly 30 years, and has broadcast both on the ABC and the Nine Network television coverage.

TONY COZIER

IT may be an overworked cliche but, for two generations of West Indians, Alan McGilvray really was the Voice of Australian cricket. In the days before television brought sport live and direct into their living rooms from the ends of the earth, he was their ears and their eyes as well.

Our school geography taught us the precise location of Australia on the map and we learned of its wheat and its sheep and its koalas and its gross domestic product. But cricket taught us much more about the character of its people and we gleaned most about the character of its cricketers from McGilvray.

By my reckoning, Alan described 52 Tests between Australia and the West Indies, spanning 11 series from 1951 to 1985. West Indians who love and know their cricket could identify Alan as a kindred spirit and it was no surprise that news of his passing prompted more than a few calls to radio sports shows in the Caribbean to recall his work.

Before ever setting eyes on Australia—or, for that matter, an Australian—I would stay awake through endless nights listening to the distinctive, clipped accents of McGilvray, and his early colleague Johnny Moyes, from far-off cities whose names were long since familiar from datelines over newspaper reports of Test matches. The crackling shortwave reception merely heightened the excitement of

Tony Cozier, popular Barbadian journalist and broadcaster, on his first visit to Australia.

Ramadhin confronting Hassett, or Benaud doing his stuff to Sobers, the regular intervention of the staccato ABC race commentaries and the mystifying announcement of 'correct weight at Randwick' further stirring young wonder.

By fortunate coincidence, my first series as radio commentator happened to be in 1965, Alan's first of three tours of the Caribbean. As a wide-eyed rookie of 25, I might have been overwhelmed by such eminent company as himself and our own dean of commentators at the time, the late Roy Lawrence, except that both were so magnanimous with their help and advice.

There were two credos McGilvray passed on then that have remained etched in my consciousness. One was, as he put it, to 'never let the crowd beat you'; the other was to 'never leave your listeners hanging'.

He considered it the height of unprofessionalism for the description of a key incident to be drowned by the reaction of the crowd. It is, of course, inevitable to miss a wicket or a dropped catch for they happen in the blink of an eye. But Alan used a simple technique to be able to be ahead of the roar.

He considered the phrase 'he bowls' at the point of delivery,

A magnificent action shot of Garfield Sobers. His century in the Tied Test in Brisbane was described by Johnny Moyes as the best innings he had seen in 50 years of watching cricket. Mac rated him one of the greatest all-rounders but found him flawed as a captain.

favoured by so many of his contemporaries, time-consuming and redundant. 'What else was the bowler running up for? was his logical question. Instead, he would transfer his attention to the batsman's end, ready for the immediate description of what would happen next. Thus: 'Davidson is on his way to Hunte and Hunte ... drives-cut-pulls-defends-edges-is bowled-caught-dropped-hit on the pad', then pausing to allow the crowd to enhance the effect—not vice versa. He seldom missed.

He was also constantly conscious of not developing a point only to have it abruptly overtaken by the play itself. It took a sense of timing that came with experience and gave rise to one of Alan's catch phrases. 'I'll get back to that' he would say as he turned his attention to immediate description, letting the listeners know he hadn't forgotten them.

His style differed markedly from the informality of the BBC team to whom the cricket often seemed incidental. He lacked the rich literary flair of John Arlott and the impish sense of humour of Brian Johnston. His was cricket through and through so that, while Arlott would dismiss a straightforward stroke as just that before returning to his poetic description of the surroundings and Johnston would be keener on who baked the latest chocolate cake than on a casual leave-alone, Alan placed great emphasis on precisely what was happening in the middle, no matter how mundane. Thus: 'Sobers is right forward to a good length leg-break and pushes it slowly two feet to Harvey's right hand at cover without the thought of a run'.

Even above the style of his commentary, Alan was most admired in the West Indies for his fearlessness and his fair-mindedness. He had been a first-class cricketer himself, had captained New South Wales and batted with Bradman and other greats of the 1930s. He didn't make a song and dance about such facts but no one could pull any wool over his eyes.

Of course, he was an Australian through and through and proud of his country's cricketing traditions and strengths. But I never knew it to cloud his judgment of the game he so obviously loved and knew so well.

The business over Charlie Griffith's action was a prominent case in point. Charlie was big, mean and fast and, with Wes Hall, comprised as menacing a bowling combination as the game has known. Arriving in the Caribbean for their 1965 tour, the Australians, under Bobby Simpson, had had first-hand experience of Wes in Australia, both in the unforgettable 1960–61 series and then in the Sheffield Shield where he played a couple of seasons with Queensland. They only knew of Griffith by reputation following his tremendous tour of England in 1963.

There had been whispers in England about the legality of his action and, it should be said, in the West Indies too. Almost as soon as he sent his trademark yorker into the blockhole and followed it with a searing bouncer in the opening salvos of the first Test, the Australians became obsessed with the issue. They were supported in

Controversial West Indies bowler Charlie Griffith. Contrary to the popularly held opinion, Mac believed his action was legal.

their view that Griffith was throwing by Richie Benaud, their revered previous Test captain, who shot dozens of pictures as evidence. They themselves spent hours filming their nemesis from every conceivable angle and then watching the results in their hotel rooms.

It was a pointless and self-defeating exercise and Alan told them so. He also told them that, as far as he was concerned, while Griffith's

Wes Hall bowled the last over in the fabulous Tied Test in Brisbane in 1960. This was the greatest cricketing moment that Mac missed. He was never to leave a cricket ground early again.

action might have been suspect, it was legitimate under the laws of the game. It needed guts to take such a stand, for Alan McGilvray was the sole representative of the Australian Broadcasting Commission and there were those who felt that, as such, he was honour bound to toe the party line.

I could sense the pressure he was under and asked him about it.

It was part of the job, he said, and he warned that, like everyone else in such positions, I would inevitably experience it as time went on and advised that anytime I felt I couldn't report what I felt to be true then I should try something else.

In spite of that, he always seemed to have an excellent rapport with everyone in the game, from administrators, to players, to fans. Whether they agreed with all of his strongly expressed views or not, they respected his sincerity and his knowledge.

By the time he first came to the Caribbean, Alan had seen West Indies cricket at first hand during the series in Australia in 1951–52 and 1960–61. As his autobiography reveals, he quickly appreciated the problems of the insularity that has always afflicted our cricket but he took a delight in the way our players approached the game.

Until the ugly incidents that marred his final Caribbean tour in 1978, he was also enraptured by the passion West Indians have for the game.

That trip was overshadowed throughout by the Packer controversy that threw international cricket into such turmoil. Like so many others of his generation, Alan was appalled that a private entrepreneur—and in Australia, to boot—could step in and entice the game's finest players away from Test cricket. His mood became even darker when the West Indies initially chose all their Packer players and expectedly steamrollered the Packerless Australians in under three days in the first two Tests.

These were difficult times for Alan, and so many others, who were witnessing first hand their great game torn asunder. Alan even suggested the West Indies' World Series players donate some of their Packer earnings to the West Indies Board as compensation for the days' gate takings lost because of the early finishes in the unequal contests.

When the inevitable split between the West Indies Board and the Packer players duly came midway through the series, the cricket was more competitive. But the public's mood was already embittered by the controversy at a time of political tension in several of the islands. The culmination was an intimidating crowd riot that prematurely ended the last Test in Jamaica with Australia on the verge of victory. As the special police, behind their helmets and batons, fired their rifles into the air and players sought the sanctuary of their dressing room, Alan later reported a frightening confrontation with some hostile elements that left him shaken and vowing never to return.

It was an unfortunate episode and Alan never spoke with the

same warmth about the Caribbean again. It was a pity for I know he developed a soft spot for the place on earlier trips.

My memories of Alan McGilvray will mostly be of a day's beach cricket on Barbados' east coast in 1965 when Everton Weekes despatched a few of his rusty medium-pacers into the Atlantic Ocean, much to Alan's delight; of indulging in a few more Mount Gay Rum and sodas than were good for us as we watched the sun set from the patio of the old Royal Hotel in Barbados; of listening spellbound as he, Gerry Gomez, Jeff Stollmeyer and Keith Miller waxed warm about the game which each, in his own way, had graced.

But, above all, to me and all West Indians, Alan McGilvray will be remembered best as the irreplaceable voice of Australian cricket.

THE change in the West Indies between Alan McGilvray's first tour in 1965 and his last in 1978 was quite marked. The idyllic nature of carefree islands had been overtaken by economic, social and racial problems that had become in many cases quite sinister. Compounding all of this in 1978 was the great schism in cricket which had followed the World Series breakaway. In the West Indies the split eventually meant the absence of their key players from a series against Australia, and to a nation which did not care a fig for cricket politics, this was greatly resented.

The riots which accompanied the Test series of 1978 to which Tony Cozier has referred led to a classic McGilvray broadcast of events as they occurred. They also soured him forever against the West Indies as a place in which Test cricket could happily be played.

The extract from The Game Is Not The Same *paints a graphic picture of the difficulties of 1978.*

ALAN McGILVRAY

The commentary box in all the Test grounds in the West Indies is directly opposite the Members' Pavilion, so each day at start and close of play, and at the adjournments if I was game enough, I had to cross the field to get to and from the box. Those short walks became increasingly harrowing. I was abused and reviled and generally made to feel most uncomfortable.

The final Test brought matters to a head. The most terrible

riot erupted on the last day. The game ended in a hail of house bricks and amidst volleys of gunfire.

It all started when Australia were pressing towards victory on the last afternoon. The West Indies had lost eight second innings wickets and still had 38 balls of the last 20 overs to play when Vanburn Holder was given out, caught by Steve Rixon at the wicket off the bowling of leg-spinner Jim Higgs. Holder stood and considered his position. There was no doubt he was out, and I think Holder lingered as much for his disappointment as for any dissatisfaction with the decision. But he did linger as if to dispute the verdict. That was enough for the crowd. Tension had been high for weeks, and the double disappointment of not having their better players, then seeing Australia in a position to win, was too much for them. Holder later was mortified that he had not left the field immediately. He simply did not consider the consequences. Holder is a good man and a very fair man, and the last thing he would want to do was in any way to trigger the sort of mayhem that followed his reluctance to leave the crease.

First of all came the missiles. There were bottles seemingly by the truckload, oil drums, chairs, bricks, literally anything that could be torn up and hurled. The bricks were travelling close to 100 metres from the perimeter of the ground. I reasoned they must have had some sort of slingshot arrangement to fire them that far.

The players gradually retreated from the pitch towards the Members' Stand. At first the former West Indies captain Gerry Alexander and the Australian manager Fred Bennett went out on to the field to try to calm things down. They had no chance.

The police joined the fray, pistols drawn. There was sporadic gunfire. Fred Bennett said later that the police had told him they were only firing blanks. I spent enough time in the army to know that blanks don't make the whistling noise I heard the bullets making that day. They were only aimed in the air, but bullets are bullets, and the fact they were fired at all emphasised the critical stage matters had reached.

When the players eventually took the decision to run for their lives, they were showered with bottles and debris. I remember describing the scene back to Australia. I said they were being rained with bottles, and it would be a miracle if someone was not seriously hurt. The only injury as it turned out was a small cut Gerry Alexander suffered to his head. The Australian players were extremely lucky.

I watched it all from the elevated broadcasting box. I had a briefcase packed with papers in front of my face as a shield as I spoke into the microphone. A crowd had gathered below us and was making it very obvious we were the enemy and what we were saying in our broadcasts was not to its liking.

Eventually the riot police arrived. They wore shields and protective gear and were armed with automatic weapons. I remember thinking: Hell, if someone pulls a trigger here it will be carnage. Thankfully the riot police were better trained than that. But for a time it was an extremely dangerous scene. Eventually we had to consider the dash across the field from the broadcasting box to the Members' Pavilion. I made several attempts to negotiate the twenty or so steps down to the ground. Waiting at the bottom were half a dozen men armed with bricks.

'You get back inside, man,' they demanded. I was in no position to argue. Half a dozen times I tried to make my way out of that box, and half a dozen times I was threatened and turned back. I apparently had upset the locals by describing the scene in some detail, and bemoaning the fact that the machine-guns were necessary at a cricket Test. I felt that my duty.

An hour passed before I even looked like getting out of the box. Jackie Hendricks, a former West Indies wicket-keeper who had been in Australia with Frank Worrell's team, was in the adjoining box. I sought his assistance in getting across the field. 'No way man,' came his reply. 'No way.' He intended staying there all night if necessary. He would not venture out while there were any remnants of the rioting mobs below.

We eventually made our break when only two or three people remained below. Once we reached the ground however, they came from everywhere. Jackie and I were separated. A mob of about forty people surrounded me, jostling and jeering. Jackie was having the same sort of trouble with a mob of his own. I used my briefcase as a sort of shield cum battering ram to get close to the Members' Pavilion, where I was rescued by a policeman.

'You crazy fool,' he rebuked me. 'You could have been knifed out there, and you wouldn't have known where it was coming from.' That, I admit, I had not considered. I was naturally very apprehensive about the whole thing, but I don't think I was actually frightened until the policeman put it like that.

The Australian players had been barricaded in their dressing room. They were still being pelted with missiles of all descriptions.

Once in the pavilion Fred Bennett grabbed hold of me. 'Come with me Mac,' he beckoned. 'We're having a meeting with the President in the committee room and I want a witness.' The President of the West Indies Board was Mr Alan Rae, and he was mightily upset by everything that had taken place. Four or five policemen flanked him and he was very agitated. His main concern was that the match be extended into the next morning so it could be completed. He reasoned it would be wrong if Australia were robbed of their winning chance. The riot had knocked the pitch around but that didn't seem to worry him. So long as they could make it playable, he wanted everybody back next morning to wrap things up.

While the debate raged I joined Jack Anderson, a well-known and very fair-minded Jamaican journalist for a much-needed drink. He was as upset about events as I was. The problem, in fact, probably bit more deeply for Jack, because he had to live with it constantly. Life in Kingston was pretty tough at that time, and the difficulties at the cricket were symptomatic of many social problems the island of Jamaica itself was confronting. Jack apologised that he had to leave. His wife was cooking him a roast, he said, and we agreed to have a farewell drink next day, since it seemed the cricket would be resumed.

The ride back to the hotel from the Kingston Ground normally was no more than ten minutes. I was driven back that evening through the mob that still lingered outside the ground. They were harrassing any car that carried an Australian. They thumped at the windows, stood in front of the vehicle, generally made things as difficult as they could. It took forty-five minutes to make the hotel.

On the way a newsflash on the radio announced that Jack Anderson had been shot and killed on the way home. I couldn't believe it. I had been drinking with him not an hour before. Whatever effect the riots had had on me to that point now paled against the horror and revulsion I felt. When I reached the hotel I rang Jack's son. He confirmed that his father was dead. He had been machine-gunned.

By now I was shaking. I don't know whether it was rage, or hate, or fear. It could have been all of those things. But to think that so simple and so honourable a pursuit as cricket, which I loved so dearly, could be surrounded by such madness made the blood run cold. I was wrestling with these emotions when I had a visitor. He introduced himself as a representative of the Australian government and without beating about the bush explained that they would like me out of Jamaica.

My reports of events, though 100 per cent accurate as far as I was concerned, did not paint the West Indies well and were considered inflammatory. And since they could not guarantee my safety, they'd rather I wasn't there. Somehow it didn't seem right and I started to argue. The cricket was to continue next day after all, and it didn't seem right to run. But he was very persuasive. I was out of the hotel early next morning and spent the hours before the first available flight in the comparative security of the airport. I was a very relieved man when that flight reached Miami, Florida.

I vowed I would never return to the West Indies. It was a heart-breaking farewell. I had met so many wonderful people there, and been entertained so often and so royally through those tours of 1965 and 1973. That it should end like this was one of the saddest experiences of my life in cricket.

BRIDGING GENERATIONS
by Ian Chappell

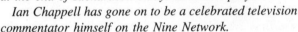

Ian Chappell was captain of Australia from 1971 to 1975, and was a very influential factor in modernising the game. His grandfather Vic Richardson was a co-commentator with Alan McGilvray at the start of his career, and their cricket careers had coincided briefly at the end of Richardson's days as a Test player.

Ian Chappell has gone on to be a celebrated television commentator himself on the Nine Network.

IAN CHAPPELL

'He'll have to hurry. And hurry he does. Australia are now in a strong position.' Those were among the first words I heard from Alan McGilvray.

As a keen cricket-following kid I used to love listening to Alan. Not just to find out how Australia in general and Keith Miller in particular were faring, but also to hear his word picture of the ground where the match was being played. In this way McGilvray was an inspiration to many kids who grew up wanting to discover if those grounds he talked about really resembled his description. There was only one way to find out and that was to play for Australia.

Having had the good fortune to play for Australia and find out for myself that the grounds really did fit McGilvray's description, it also gave me the opportunity to meet the man. I found Alan to be good company, a patriotic Australian and helpful to me.

First, I discovered I had an ally in Alan. This probably came about because he'd spent so much time commentating with my grandfather Vic Richardson. Mac would occasionally talk to me about his days in the broadcasting box with Vic; how he enjoyed them and how he'd learned a lot from Vic. It was thanks to Alan's perception and persuasion that I enjoyed a happy evening with my grandfather not long before he died.

I was attending an award ceremony in early 1969 and the sponsors had kindly flown Vic and my father Martin to Sydney to be part of the presentation. As we celebrated at the bar after the award, Mac suggested that we pay Vic's great mate Alan Kippax a late night visit.

Alan Kippax rekindled memories of Victor Trumper with his classical batting style. He was put on a pedestal by the young McGilvray, who was a schoolboy at Sydney Grammar in the 1920s.

Vic agreed it was a good idea and after we eventually found Kippax's house we spent an enjoyable few hours chatting. This was the last time the two old mates saw each other, which helped to make the night something special in my memory.

I also remember the evening well because it confirmed that my grandfather's circle of mates was widespread. As a young player touring Australia, England and South Africa, many people came up to me and said, 'I knew your grandfather Vic.' In particular, hundreds of people told me they were actually there late one night when Vic took a famous ride on the pie cart through the streets of Adelaide. So you can imagine I was a bit sceptical about some of these 'mates of Vic'.

However, this night we took off for Kippax's house in a taxi, only armed with the name of the street and not the house number. McGilvray was confident he had recognised Kippax's house and so the cabbie was duly paid off, but unfortunately he'd chosen the wrong house. So we spread out in search of the place, armed only with a description from Mac, which in no way ranked with those of the cricket grounds he'd talked about in my youth.

Vic eventually thought he'd sighted the place and called McGilvray over to investigate. With that a window flew up and a guy in pyjamas poked his head out and said, 'Will you noisy bastards shut ... Hey, is that you Vic?'

Vic stopped in his tracks and after peering into the dark for a few seconds replied, 'Is that you Robbo?'

'Gawd strike me lucky, Victor bloody Richardson,' declared Robbo. He happened to be an old mate from the services and before you could say Jack Robinson, we were in the kitchen drinking a beer. That is when I realised that a hell of a lot of people *did* know Vic Richardson. A few years ago Alan McGilvray was answering questions at a function to celebrate the reunion of the 1973 Australian side that won in the Caribbean. During one of his answers Mac said, 'There is a lot of Victor York (Richardson) in Ian Chappell.' That is a tribute I treasure.

It was a few years before our successful tour of the Caribbean that I discovered Mac was not only good company, but he was actually *dangerously* good company. We were touring South Africa and Doug Walters, Brian Taber and I suddenly decided around midnight that we would wake McGilvray for a drink. As we had about a 30 year age advantage it seemed like a good idea at the time. However, when Mac unscrewed the top on the scotch bottle and tossed it out the window we suspected our plan was flawed. Our suspicions were confirmed

Ian Chappell's sensational catch in his first Test for Australia in 1964 was a great thrill for his grandfather Vic Richardson, who had been recalled by the ABC as a guest commentator for the match.

when he followed with the words, 'Now we have to drink until the bottle is finished.'

There were moments when the dulcet tones of McGilvray didn't soothe the nerves of all Australians. Nevertheless, there was never any doubt about where Mac's loyalties lay. An impartial broadcaster he certainly was, but in the right circumstances you discovered he was first and foremost a proud Australian. On the previous tour of South Africa in 1966–67, we had been beaten at the Wanderers in Johannesburg to become the first Australian side to lose a Test in that country. We then took a pounding in the third encounter at Old Kings-mead in Durban. During this match one of the more arrogant South African supporters kept jumping up and down in front of the commentary box and poking fun at the Australian side. Mac could only take so much before he threw open the window and told the gentleman, 'Sir, I can understand you becoming excited as South Africa have only beaten Australia once in this country, but would you mind not obstructing our view from the commentary box.'

The more you got to know Mac, the more you understood his love of cricket and knowledge of broadcasting. He loved to sit down and talk cricket with the players. He would expound his theories, listen to the players and any appropriate tidbits he gleaned he would weave into his story the next day. He also possessed a cricketer's ability to look past the play on the field and tell the listener not just what was happening, but why it was occurring.

Mac was responsible for making cricket broadcasting a respectable profession. Thanks to him there are now many opportunities for an ex-cricketer to continue his life 'in the game', as not only did Mac inspire youngsters to want to play on those international fields, he did

Doug Walters drives majestically. Patrick Eagar

Brian Taber, pictured here, joined Ian Chappell and Doug Walters in a midnight visit to Mac—a stunt that backfired.

his job so well he made it possible for them to pursue a career in cricket broadcasting.

I guess it is also true to say Alan had some influence on my captaincy. Over a beer in Sydney in late 1969 he confided that an influential Australian Cricket Board (ACB) official had told him, 'because of his actions in South Africa, Chappell will never captain Australia'. That official obviously didn't wield as much power as he thought, because less than six months later I was appointed captain.

When Mac visited Vic Richardson in Adelaide he may well have encountered the determined, formidable stance of the young Ian Chappell.

My 'action in South Africa' had been to vote against Australia playing an extra Test. This proposed match had belatedly been added to the tour itinerary, replacing two first-class games that were scheduled to be played after the fourth Test. Fortunately, this meant our tour contract had to be extended by a couple of days and I saw this as the players' opportunity to take a stand. We had been shafted by the ACB at every turn on this tour. First, there was the three month tour of India where we didn't stay in the best hotels available and then we travelled to South Africa with virtually no time to acclimatise to totally different pitches. As far as I was concerned this was a chance to stand up and say, 'We are tired of being pushed around without having a voice in the matter.'

As a team we were appalled at the lack of consideration for our well-being shown by our Board during the Indian tour. Following a team discussion our captain Bill Lawry decided to sit down and write a letter to the ACB putting forward our complaints. Near the end of the South African tour, as vice-captain I asked Bill if he had written the letter. He replied that he was in the process. I suggested he finish it before the end of the tour so that we all had the opportunity to sign the letter. However, Bill decided that he alone would sign the letter. I have always felt that his reign as captain was doomed from the day the ACB received his communique.

When I heard of my appointment as captain, it was the knowledge of what Mac had told me, my gut feeling about Bill's demise and the thoughtless way the Board allowed Lawry to discover through the media that he'd lost the job, that led me to say, 'the bastards won't get me like that'. In that way my view of the captaincy had been shaped and I was always going to be for the players. McGilvray certainly didn't agree with all that happened in cricket in the 1970s. He believed it was more a gentleman's game to be played competitively, but the realist in him also allowed that the world was changing fast. True to himself McGilvray would praise what he thought was good about the game and place on record what he disliked. That was the good thing about Mac, you always knew where you stood.

Not only was he good company on tour, he was like having an extra man. In the days before spectators booked on tours to support their team it was comforting to know that we always had someone who was on our side even if he couldn't cheer in the commentary box. Equally, Mac was grateful for the company of cricketers on tour.

In the early part of the 1973 tour of the Caribbean his usually up-beat approach to life was not in evidence. He'd received the bad news that his beloved wife Gwen was ill and if it hadn't been for his strong sense of duty, I am sure he would have left the tour. He did tell me at one stage that this would be his last tour. Fortunately he changed his mind after Gwen died, as I think cricket was good for Mac after that devastating loss.

Unfortunately, I didn't see as much of Alan as I would have liked once he retired from broadcasting. However, there were still a few memorable occasions. I recall him telling me at the SCG that a former player had advised him to give up smoking. 'What, at age 82 and add an extra ten seconds to my life?' Mac had replied. 'Don't be so absurd.'

Sadly, the next time I saw him was in hospital after he'd broken his pelvis following a fall off a ladder while he was doing some gardening. He wouldn't have been the ideal patient, but he did recover sufficiently to leave hospital and fight a few more battles.

Not long after he left hospital I read a long piece in the Sydney Morning Herald, where Mac said he was ready to die as it was time to be reunited with Gwen. I thought to myself that it sounded sad, but then I realised that it was typical McGilvray right to the end; telling it like it was.

It certainly won't be the same in cricket circles without Alan McGilvray's company.

Alan Kippax was captain of the NSW team when the young Alan McGilvray first made the Shield side, and his influence on McGilvray was marked. They lived not far from each other, and their friendship endured in the post cricket years. Kippax and Victor Richardson were also close, and the account of their late night meeting which Ian Chappell has given is in keeping with the spontaneous manner in which they enjoyed each other's company.

In The Games Goes On, *however, McGilvray recounts a somewhat deeper purpose to their late night visit to the Kippax household, and an attendant benefit for the young Australian captain-to-be . . .*

ALAN McGILVRAY

Early in Ian Chappell's career I recall a rather remarkable coaching session which I am sure did the future Australian captain little harm.

Ian was quite young and had come to Sydney for a function in one of the leading hotels. His grandfather, Vic Richardson, was with him. Vic and I had long been friends, since the days we played against each other and through years together in the ABC commentary team, along with Arthur Gilligan. When the function was over Vic and Ian came back to my home, to continue the mood as it were, with just an odd drink or two to round off the evening.

The subject, needless to say, was cricket, and when Alan Kippax's name came up Vic decided the proper thing to do was to bring him into the conversation. Vic was one of those gregarious, impulsive fellows who had few inhibitions when it came to his mates. The fact that it was nigh on midnight and that Kippie would have been long bedded down didn't deter him an inch.

Off we all traipsed to the Kippax household, which was not all that far from my place, and Vic hammered on the door until his old team-mate could rouse himself and stagger into a dressing gown. I have often wondered why Kippie didn't simply throw us out, and all our good cheer with us, but I suppose he was too much of a gentleman for that, and he was pleased to see Vic, anyway.

As we carried on our party in the Kippax kitchen, Ian happened to remark that Vic had been telling him what a great cutter of the ball Kippax had been. We could all testify to that. He used to clip the wicket-keeper's gloves with his bat on occasions, so late did he play the ball, and he once nominated to me, batting at the other end, that he would cut the ball past each of the slip fieldsmen in turn. He did, too, such was his control.

Ian Chappell obviously was keen to learn and, despite the late hour and broken sleep, Kippie was keen to help. He went to the broom cupboard, produced a broom and began to play in his kitchen some of the most articulate strokes you would ever want to see. The young Chappell was engrossed. He checked the placement of his hands, watched the shift of his body weight and the deft placement of feet. He took it all in.

It was a quite ridiculous scene, really. Kippax in pyjamas playing aristocratic cuts, his dressing gown flowing, and the young up-and-comer lapping it up. But it proved a few things. It proved how important the batting art was to Kippax and how the grace of a former age had been worked at and perfected, quite apart from natural gifts. It proved how much Ian Chappell wanted to learn and improve his game and that the extraordinary value he later proved to the Australian cause was no coincidence. And it proved the value of experience, passed on by whatever means available, to any player in any age.

This, to me, was the art of cricket, no matter how incongruous the setting, or how late the hour.

McGilvray, through his broadcasts and his writing, left little doubt that he considered Ian Chappell to be the most effective of all the Australian captains whom he had seen in action. This was largely due to Chappell's competitive edge, and to the fact that he had a particular talent for drawing the ultimate performance from the men around him. He had a capacity for demanding loyalty which McGilvray admired greatly.

The natural link between Chappell and McGilvray had grown from the fact that Chappell was Vic Richardson's grandson. But ultimately McGilvray made his judgments without any peripheral influence, and he rated Chappell as a captain for his deeds alone, for his imagination, for his aggression, and for his fiercely determined commitment to winning. This extract from Captains Of The Game *enunciates the influence which McGilvray considered Chappell to have had on the modern game.*

A case undoubtedly could be made to paint Ian Chappell as the most influential cricketer of the Australian game. Not just for his batting, which was full of grit and fight and marvellously productive, nor just for his captaincy, although, in terms of getting a team to perform to its full potential, and perhaps beyond, it ranks above any other in my experience. The lasting influence Ian Chappell has had on cricket, I believe, is as a conduit between eras. His abrasiveness, his single-mindedness and his rebelliousness created an atmosphere in which great change came quickly, and a game that had remained relatively untouched in character for half a century or more was transformed.

A lot of people regret that change, of course, from the gentle ways of old to some of the less dignified attitudes of today. I do myself in many ways. But it was probably inevitable that cricket would have to modify its pace and its outlook to fit into a more commercial and less patient modern world.

Ian Chappell became the cricketing symbol of a restless generation. He brought to the Australian captaincy an individuality unlike anything that had gone before. He spoke out when he thought things had to be said. He cast off the conservative image of the white shirt and tie and presented himself for cricketing duty as if he was off to the local disco. He would neither tolerate fools nor toe any official line he considered to be humbug. And in Chappell's time, at the end of the revolutionary 1960s, it has to be said there was a fair bit of official humbug around. Chappell was of the era of moon landings and colour TV. He had little patience for standards and conventions which he thought belonged to the age of the crystal wireless.

In Chappell's time at the top of Australian cricket the game jumped from a sleepy period dominated at the Test level by laborious scoring and drawn games, into a golden age for Australian Test cricket. Names like Dennis Lillee, Greg Chappell, Doug Walters, Rod Marsh and the rest provided the best entertainment for a decade or so and the biggest crowds, consistently, since the days of Bradman some thirty years before. By the time all the convulsions were over, Chappell was leading a team which played in yellow clothes, bowling a white ball under huge night lights before capacity crowds. For many, it was a different game altogether.

Chappell's attitudes may or may not have triggered that revolution. But they certainly created the environment in which it could succeed. And when it came, Chappell was leading it from the front, and happy to let the devil take the hindmost.

A MATTER OF TIMING

by Norman May

Norman May headed the ABC's television cricket commentary team from 1970 to 1985. Prior to that he had been a cricket commentator on ABC Radio, as well as establishing himself as the 'all-rounder' of national sporting commentary. For many years he presented the ABC Sportsman of the Year Award, and achieved enduring fame as the most passionate of broadcasters at Olympic and Commonwealth Games.

NORMAN MAY

Saturday, 15 November 1958, was a memorable day in my broadcasting life. It was the occasion of my first ever cricket broadcast and also, it was the first time I had worked in the same commentary team as the man I regarded then (and still do) as the greatest of all cricket commentators, Alan McGilvray.

I was rostered second in a team of three commentators. This meant that I was scheduled to replace Alan 20 minutes after the start of play, and as an absolute novice about to follow an internationally famous commentator, I had a very bad case of butterflies in the tummy.

The match was NSW versus the touring MCC team under the captaincy of Peter May. In those days all minor matches were played as the MCC (Marylebone Cricket Club) and only the Test matches were played as England.

My memories of the game are quite sketchy. The MCC, batting first, had been dismissed for less than 200 on the Friday. On the fateful Saturday, NSW batted all day and beyond to set up a sizeable first innings lead. Outstanding for NSW were Neil Harvey and Jim Burke, who both scored centuries, and Norman O'Neill who played an entertaining innings of 84 not out. The MCC recovered in the second innings and the match finished in a draw.

Norman May aged 30 in 1958. A former beach inspector who turned broadcaster.

My most vivid recollection was of the sick feeling in the pit of my stomach when I entered the broadcast box for the first time. At the end of the over, Alan brought the score up to date and then said: 'Your next commentator is Peter May.'

It was a straight-out case of mistaken identity. Fortunately, I saw the humour of the situation and it had the effect of making me forget about my own nervous problems and I managed to stumble through the next 20 minutes without any major slip-ups.

As a point of interest, Peter May asked me about my surname some years later. I explained that my father was English. He had lived in South London and had migrated to Australia while still in his teens. Peter, who played for Surrey, agreed that there was a slight chance we could be related.

After I finished my first broadcasting stint, Alan was waiting for me outside the box. He apologised most sincerely and he said 'Look I know your name is *Norman* May. I shan't make the same mistake again.' I said not to worry and that I was in a slightly more confident frame of mind for my next session. The next time around, Alan made

Peter May (England) and Richie Benaud (Australia)—rival captains in Australia in 1958–59. The Australians confounded the experts by winning the Ashes by the decisive margin of four Tests to nil.

the cross and he said 'Your next commentator is Norman O'Neill.' True to his word, Alan had not made the same mistake twice. Remarkably, Alan and I were associated for more than a quarter of a century, and in all of those years, I never heard of him making a similar error with other commentators' names. In retrospect, it was quite flattering to be named firstly as England's captain and then as one of Australia's most dynamic batsmen.

A couple of weeks later, another memorable occasion was my first ever cricket telecast, and once again Alan and I were co-commentators. I'm fairly certain it was Alan's first telecast as well. He had always concentrated on radio and right from the start, he showed a reluctance to work on television.

It was a Saturday afternoon grade match at Mosman Oval. The local team Mosman was involved and I can't remember the other team. But I can recall that it was my turn to make an embarrassing blunder. It was a cloudy, overcast day with the possibility of rain. Soon after the start of the telecast, Alan asked me a question on air. He said 'Norman, you used to be a beach inspector. Do you think it will rain?'

It was true; I had been a beach inspector for one season at Fresh-water Beach on Sydney's north side, not too far away from Mosman

Oval. In reply to Alan's question, I gave what I thought was a learned dissertation on the weather outlook. I said the clouds were high and that the breeze was a nor'-easter, the prevailing wind in Sydney, and not usually a rain producer. I concluded it would not rain under these conditions. Those were famous last words. In about 10 minutes, it started to come down in bucket loads. The rain was as heavy as I've seen at a cricket ground in Sydney and in half an hour, play was abandoned for the day, and the remainder of the telecast was cancelled.

Alan and I adjourned to the Oaks Hotel at Neutral Bay and while we were sipping an ice cold beer, he gave me the first of many helpful hints on cricket broadcasting. He said: 'Never try to forecast what might happen in a game of cricket. If you do, you'll discover that you'll be wrong seven or eight times out of ten. Leave the forecasting to someone else.' I replied 'Mr Mac, I'm not going to forecast what might happen in the cricket, and after today, I'm not going to forecast the weather either.' And I've stuck to that promise right through to the present day.

The Oaks Hotel at Neutral Bay is a favourite haunt for cricketers. In later years, the corner room was re-named the Doug Walters Bar, and of course 'Dashing Douglas' was one of Alan's great cricketing mates. Another regular was the well known actor, the late John Meillon, who was something of a cricket fanatic.

For the series between England and Australia in 1958–59, Alan was the No 1 radio commentator and I was employed as a script writer for the daily films on television. In those days, television was still in its infancy in Australia and there was no link between the capital cities, and in some cases, such as Brisbane and Adelaide, television had not even started. So the Test matches were shot on 16 mm film which was flown daily to Sydney for editing and recording. The radio commentary was my only source of information and it provided me with an excellent opportunity to study Alan's work from a technical viewpoint.

In this series, I learned a surprising fact about Test cricket. The cinecameraman could cover the whole of the critical action in the day's play by exposing 3400 feet of 16 mm film. This was about 90 minutes, and it meant that nothing actually happened for about four of the five and a half hours of scheduled play. Changing ends between overs; the bowler walking back to his mark; the setting of fields and other delays, all added up to about 70 per cent of the available action.

In addition, that series was one of the slowest and dreariest ever played with Richie Benaud's young Australians begrudging every run to win the Ashes by the clear margin of four Tests to nil, despite the fact that England appeared to have one of its strongest ever teams on paper. England's overall scoring rate of 33.23 runs per 100 balls was the lowest since 1886 and the second lowest in history. In the first Test in Brisbane, England scored only 19 before lunch and a miserly 141 in the whole day's play. Trevor Bailey's 68 in just under six hours remains the slowest half century ever scored in England–Australia Tests. With all of these factors combined, the broadcasting of these matches was an extremely difficult task. I marvelled at Alan's ability to maintain his enthusiasm and he never seemed to be padding.

Most of the other commentators were clearly in trouble. At the end of the series, I asked Alan about the broadcasting problems. He was a man who rarely swore or used bad language. He summed it up in a very curt reply: 'Bloody hard!' Those two words said it all.

In contrast, the next series in Australia has been described as the greatest ever played. This was the fabulous Tied Test series against the West Indies in 1960–61. Compared to England's 19 before lunch and 141 in a full day, the West Indies scored 130 before lunch and 359 by stumps on the first day of the Brisbane Test. This match finished in a tie, the first in Test match history. It set the tempo for a marvellous series of five Tests which completely erased the bitter memories of the stodgy series against England two years before.

Alan has often told the story of his decision to leave the Brisbane ground to catch an early flight home. He thought the match would finish in a draw and he didn't even know the result until he arrived at Sydney airport. I heard the live broadcast of the final over, and without being too critical of the commentators involved, I'm certain that Alan McGilvray would have made a better fist of it. In 1961, Alan was 51 years old, and at this stage, I believed he was right at the peak of his career. Like many famous broadcasters, his greatest asset was his voice. It was rich and vibrant, and I felt that everything he said was totally convincing and believable. Probably the most important thing was that his voice was distinctive and he was immediately recognised as Alan McGilvray and no one else. I regard this as an essential requirement for success in broadcasting.

Also, he could vary his delivery to suit any situation. In the fourth Test in Adelaide, 'Slasher' MacKay and Lindsay Kline had to bat for over 100 minutes to save the match. For this broadcast Alan shortened his sentences and spoke in low register to exactly reflect the drama and tension of that last wicket partnership. Then, in the final Test in Melbourne, he put an excited edge on his voice and once again he was able to mirror the feelings of the crowd as the match, and the series, headed to a nailbiting finish. There was substantial variation in his method of delivery in those Test matches and in each case his approach was just right for the occasion.

A major change came in 1970 when Australia-wide telecasts of Test cricket were introduced for the first time. In the summer of 1970–71 the series was played between Australia and Ray Illingworth's team from England. Another important change was the awarding of a Test match to Perth, and it's fair to say that those fully national telecasts completely altered the public perception of cricket in Australia. Because of the time difference, the match from Perth was shown live in eastern Australia up until 9 o'clock at night. Cricket attracted record ratings and it's a system which has been maintained ever since; these days with Channel 9 replacing the ABC as the originating network.

I was chosen as a national TV cricket commentator and from 1970 right through to 1985, a period of 15 summers, I travelled around Australia with Alan McGilvray. It was a very happy working arrangement. We were good friends and there was never any suggestion of professional rivalry because Alan was radio and I was television.

Alan's reluctance to work on television was interesting. He received plenty of offers but he always refused, and I believe that he made the right decision. Television doesn't allow the same freedom of expression as radio. With so many action replays, television comments are governed by the production pattern, and Alan, an old dog on radio, would have difficulty in adjusting to the new tricks of television.

During this latter period of his career we had many discussions on broadcasting technique and Alan had very definite views on this subject. He believed it was essential for a commentator to be right up with the action and he regarded the bat hitting the ball as the critical point in his description. In his method, whatever the batsman did— either drove, hooked, cut or played defensively—the operative word should coincide with the sound of the bat hitting the ball. In this way, the commentator could never be beaten by the reaction of the crowd if something exciting happened.

The obvious flaw in this technique is that there is very little time

A youthful McGilvray in the early 1950s. Not as yet bespectacled, but even then, one of the rare cricket broadcasters who used field glasses.

to describe the flight of the ball before it reaches the batsman. In sequence, the ball leaves the bowler's hand, it travels briefly through the air and the batsman plays a shot. At 90 mph (144 kph), the ball takes about .45 of a second before it reaches the batsman, and with a slow bowler, maybe half a second longer. The commentator only has time for one or two words in this period, depending on the speed of the ball. Alan countered by saying that the flight could be described in retrospect. Of course, if the batsman missed or the ball hit his pads, then the ball itself could be described.

Here are two sample commentaries; firstly describing the correct sequence of action: 'Davidson runs in and bowls, it's short outside the off stump—O'Neill cuts and it could be four.'

This commentary is about two seconds behind the action and the crowd reaction has beaten the commentator. By the time the word 'cuts' is spoken, the ball has travelled about two-thirds of the way to the boundary.

Now the McGilvray method: 'Davidson runs in and bowls, O'Neill cuts a short pitched ball and it could be four.'

Here the operative word 'cut' coincides with the sound of the bat hitting the ball and the commentator has beaten the crowd.

Some purists might object to this method of broadcasting out of sequence, but it was hard to argue with a person who could be the most successful commentator in the history of the game.

It was a technique requiring concentration and speed of mental reflex. By pin-pointing the contact between bat and ball, I have heard him call batsman out caught in slips before there was any reaction from the crowd. Also, he was fortunate that his eyesight never seemed to let him down. If there were any problems, he never mentioned them. As long as I knew him, he always wore spectacles, and unlike most cricket commentators, he used field glasses as well.

In all, Alan McGilvray broadcast cricket for more than 50 years, and he continued well past the normal age of retirement. In many ways, the ABC was a public service organisation, and there was a suggestion in the mid '70s that he should give up and make way for a younger commentator. He was 65 on the tour of England in 1975. In that year, an ABC middle manager, looking for moral support, said to me that Alan was getting old, and he was losing his punch. My reply was that his worst was twice as good as anybody else's best.

The subject was never raised again.

Alan was a couple of months short of his 76th birthday when he finally retired at the end of the tour of England in 1985.

Finally, the question of his place in history. The only challengers to the title of 'best ever' are the Englishman John Arlott, and to a lesser extent, Charles Fortune of South Africa. I emphasise that I am referring to radio only. Television requires different techniques and I believe that these commentators should be judged separately.

Charles Fortune was a flamboyant, highly entertaining commentator who affected people differently. The head of the South African broadcasting organisation said once of Charles Fortune that people either loved him or hated him, there was no half measure. So for that reason, I'll discard him first of all from the list of three.

A man who did have universal appeal was John Arlott, with his quaint Hampshire accent, his splended command of the English language and his wry sense of humour. Arlott had only one slight failing; his knowledge of the game and its tactics was inferior to Alan McGilvray's. But for the casual listener hoping for entertainment in the commentary, then John Arlott was the man.

Alan McGilvray was a cricketer's commentator. He never tried to be funny—it wasn't his nature. His knowledge and judgment were outstanding and for any listener who really loved the game, Alan was the man. If cricket commentary was an Olympic sport, Alan McGilvray, for mine, would be a certain gold medallist.

The tour by Peter May's team in 1958–59—the tour which first brought Alan McGilvray and Norman May together in the commentary box— was a turning point in the Australian game. It was the series in which

The two Normans: Norman May and Norm O'Neill. Mac was there in spirit on this afternoon in September 1996 when the pair got together in Paddington's Lord Dudley Hotel—Mac's favoured drinking spot. Martin Webby (ABC)

Richie Benaud first took over the Australian team, and the devastatingly slow play that opened the series in Brisbane provided a considerable challenge for Benaud to restore cricket's entertainment value. For a commentator, the war of attrition in which the England team indulged—and notably Trevor Bailey, who later became a commentary colleague of McGilvray—presented great challenges of invention. McGilvray wrote of the trials involved in The Game Goes On.

ALAN McGILVRAY

The first Test of May's tour was the first to be televised in Australia and Bailey managed to turn it into one of the most painfully boring in the history of the game. Bailey scored at about nine runs per hour as he crawled to 68 in more than seven and a half hours. Jimmy Burke refused to be outdone by such inertia, and actually managed for Australia 28 runs in 250 minutes, which was even slower. When one day's play produced only 106 runs, I could imagine television sets being turned off everywhere and the game set back years. To broadcast such an innings was a trial of mammoth proportions. Every ball was 'back to the bowler'. It became an ordeal of imagination for us, for we virtually had to ignore the cricket and talk about all manner of things to try to make it interesting. To do that, hour after hour, is not easy.

The poetic justice of the situation dawned on me years later when Trevor Bailey joined us on the BBC commentary team. He became very entertaining then. Whenever he produced the mildest criticism of somebody taking his time at the crease, Brian Johnston and John Arlott and the rest of us let him have it with both barrels. Trevor Bailey has paid publicly many times on radio for the boredom to which he consigned us in the fifties. He will continue to be reminded of it for as long as those of us who were there at the time are around to remember. Trevor takes it all in good humour, for he is a good chap with a dry sense of humour. And for all his slowness, he was respected as a fine opponent, as is anybody who proves so hard to shift.

Trevor Bailey interviewed by Alec Bedser. 'Barnacle' Bailey, notorious in Australia for being one of the slowest batsmen in history, later became an expert commentator with the BBC, sharing many sessions with Mac.

Television was never a proposition for McGilvray. He found it limiting, restricting his word pictures to the whim of camera angles and the changing pictures. He felt much more in control when he could tell the whole story on radio. He explained it thus, in The Game Is Not The Same:

Radio offered the opportunity to present word pictures as we saw them, without restrictions. The broadcasting boxes were always harmonious places in which all the broadcasters I knew had a real desire to communicate with their public. When television entered the picture, I could not see it ever providing commentators with that same scope for expression. The ABC asked me to do television, but I declined. I tried it a couple of times, but I hated having my commentary governed by the direction a camera happened to be pointing.

On one such occasion I noticed a commotion on the SCG Hill and suggested to the producer's assistant they might train the cameras on it. 'Ten o'clock,' I yelled, to give him the angle. He looked at his watch and said it was four o'clock. I just shook my head. The same fellow had a pad in front of him and was continually playing noughts and crosses. 'Who are you playing with?' I said. 'Myself,' came the reply. 'Do you ever win?' I inquired. 'Yes, occasionally,' he said. I decided there and then my future was not in television.

THE ENGLISH EXPERIENCE
by Peter Baxter

Peter Baxter of BBC Radio Sport has shared the commentary box in England with all the greats, and unreservedly qualifies Alan McGilvray among them. It was a place for high grade professionalism ... but it was also a place for fun.

PETER BAXTER

I have a cherished memory of Alan McGilvray in late August 1985, sitting in the sunshine at the doorway of the radio commentary box at the Oval, with a pile of letters and cards on his lap and an expression on his face that spoke volumes about the affectionate nature of the farewells. For this was his last day's Test match commentary. We made sure that he had the last session of commentary, too, though for a proud Australian to have to describe a defeat at the hands of the old enemy may not have been such a privilege.

He was, for him, affected by traces of emotion that day, though from this consummate professional you could not have told easily. Maybe it was only then that he had fully realised how popular he was with British listeners. They admired his impartiality on the air, the thoroughness of his descriptions and his understanding of the players, even if many modern practices were condemned as he freely confessed to being 'a square'. Fierce though his patriotism undoubtedly was, he would never have used—on the air—the word 'we' to describe one side in a match, as has become a modern trend in broadcasters. He would plant his elbows on either side of the microphone stand on the commentary bench, raise his binoculars (with the label threatening dire consequences to anyone bold enough to tinker with the setting) and in quiet, matter-of-fact tones describe exactly and fully what he saw. The truth, the whole truth and nothing but the truth. If the action outpaced the description, it did not ruffle him. 'I'll go back on that' he would say and fill in the detail on an incident along the way.

The understanding of players was innate. He could see a captain's concern for one of his men. 'Gee, I really liked that action of Gatting's', I remember, as a batting partner was steadied at a crucial moment. That understanding certainly transcended international boundaries. It was the feeling of professional for fellow professional. And that is what the British audience loved him for.

Yet Alan McGilvray was not a great lover of Poms.

On Alan's first tour of England with that great Australian team of 1948 under Bradman, he was to join a newly formed BBC commentary team of Rex Alston, who had joined the BBC during the war as an administrator, become a broadcaster, but was now essentially cricket producer and leading commentator; EW Swanton, who had done his first commentaries before the war and now had only recently returned from a Japanese prisoner-of-war camp; and John Arlott, who had joined the BBC from the police force towards the end of the war. Arlott had been discovered as a cricket broadcaster the previous English summer, covering India's tour for the BBC World Service.

Alan followed the Australians round the country circuit in the build-up to the Test series, usually sharing facilities with a BBC commentator. In one of the early matches he had just done a broadcast with Rex Alston, which had been overheard by John Arlott at another game. Afterwards Arlott was talking down the line to Alston, evidently unaware that McGilvray still had his headphones on. 'What on earth have you got there, Rex?' was the enquiry that Alan heard, before he had even met the BBC's new commentary discovery. It was an indiscretion that was to poison their relationship permanently, though it never obviously spilled onto the airwaves. Each of these two great—but very different—broadcasters found it very hard to be gracious about the other.

The BBC commentary box in 1948 must have been a more stuffy place than it became later. I believe that Alan never felt fully accepted in it then. In 1953, anyway, it was Bernie Kerr who represented the ABC and in 1956, Michael Charlton, who was later to earn more fame in current affairs broadcasting. But for the next nine tours Alan McGilvray's was the Australian voice in the radio team. What made the BBC box a more welcoming place for him was the advent, at the start of the 1970s of Brian Johnston from the television box.

Brian Johnston, Eton, Oxford and the Guards, was, one might well say, the archetypal upper-class Pom. Not, you would think, the sort of person to make a suburban Sydney-sider feel at home. But he did. Now Alan enjoyed being included in the Johnstonian teasing. 'Mac' everywhere in Australia received the usual Johnners treatment and became 'Magillers' in England. Their approach was, of course, totally different. Brian, the genial extrovert, who made his commentary stints more of a variety act, contrasted with the factual rhythm of the McGilvray commentary. And Magillers became—like everyone else—fair game for the string of practical jokes. Most famously is remembered the occasion when, as the studio announcer was handing back to Lord's, Brian noticed that Alan had just put a large chunk of fruit cake into his mouth.

'To find out if Australia are going to get those runs they need, let's go back to Lord's and Brian Johnston,' said the man in the studio.

'Well,' said Brian, 'I think the best person to answer that is Alan McGilvray.' There was a spluttering and a shower of crumbs as Alan, conscientious as ever, tried in vain to get himself into a position to speak, while Brian was convulsed in mirth.

During another Test match, at Edgbaston, this time, the commentary team was engaged in a lengthy discussion during a rainy afternoon. The subject came up of mothers who had coached their sons. WG Grace's mother is mentioned in Wisden, with three off-spring who played for England and Brian also brought up David

Brian Johnston and Vic Marks in the BBC Test Match Special commentary box at Lord's in 1991. Patrick Eagar

Gower's mother, who had bowled to the future England captain in the garden. 'And I believe,' said Brian, 'that Penny Cowdrey's swingers were unplayable.' He then collapsed in a fit of the giggles which were so infectious. His colleagues at the microphone were similarly convulsed and so Brian tried to move the conversation along by saying, 'I believe the Chappell brothers may have been given some early coaching by their mother, who, of course was Vic Richardson's daughter. Maybe old Magillers can confirm that.'

He turned round to see Alan, slumped in a chair at the back of the box, fast asleep.

'Oh,' he said, lamely, 'I'm afraid Alan has—er—just slipped out of the box.' And he promptly dissolved again in laughter.

All this woke the sleeper, who opened his eyes with a rather disoriented and far from sotto voce, 'Eh? What was that? Is someone wanting me?'

By this time the hilarity in the box was general and in danger of requiring a return to the studio, but somehow we recovered, though I'm not sure that Alan ever fully appreciated the humour. In fact I believe that he viewed us sometimes with avuncular and bemused disapproval. But he would play his part in the Johnstonian era in the general irreverance of proceedings.

Occasionally we would hear the protest, 'Don't take me too far', which suggested that we had, perhaps, overstepped the mark. We could take his impartiality off the air too far as well. Utterly unbiased he may have been at the microphone, but he was a fierce patriot. I remember in 1981, when Australia were heading for a defeat at Old Trafford and they had just lost their seventh second innings wicket still more than 180 short of their distant victory target. Henry Blofeld was on the commentary. 'That really does seem to be the last nail in Australia's coffin,' he said.

A growl came from the seats at the back of the commentary box. 'We're not dead yet,' said a distinctly disgruntled McGilvray.

But I would not want to give the impression that tours of England were a problem for him. Apart from the welcome he always received from the listeners, he had many old friends in Britain. Visits to Sussex were always a delight to him. He had been a great friend of the old Sussex and England captain Arthur Gilligan, who had worked with him as an expert comments man on the radio. The friendship extended to the other members of the Gilligan family, so that no tour of England was complete without looking them up.

For me it was interesting at last to see him in action on his native heath, though when I first did so it was in Perth in 1982 and, as he was quick to point out, he was a long way from home. (The feature I remember most about our meeting there was the McGilvray-ism familiar to many of his friends: 'We can throw away the stopper from the bottle—we won't be needing that again.') In Melbourne, too, he grumbled to me that he was too far from Sydney (while tucking into a dozen Sydney oysters). Thus it was best to see him at a barbecue at his own place in Double Bay. A generous host surrounded by several of his old cricket friends, enjoying a yarn or two. I have another treasured memory of the BBC commentators' dinner in Sydney at the end of the 1982–83 tour, which Alan had been unable to attend. But he came along at the end with his old friend, Col Egar, for coffee and liqueurs. At one end of the table I saw this splendid scene of those two in deep and animated conversation with Fred Trueman and Trevor Bailey, sorting out the reputations of the past as well as the perceived problems of the present.

Alan, as I have said, held his hand up to being an 'old square' and not always approving all the current trends in cricket. He liked a cricketer to look like a cricketer and recalled the neatness in turn-out of some of the old-time greats like Wally Hammond 'walking out to bat between the flower-beds that used to be in front of the Sydney Members' Stand, with a corner of blue silk handkerchief just peeping out of his pocket'. Players in trainers, T-shirts and helmets did not meet with his favour.

Broadcasting, too, had moved on from those heady days of his first summary of a day's play and the remarkably enterprising piece of ground-breaking in the synthetic Test commentaries of 1938. Thirty second reports on a day's play were not his cup of tea at all. Nor was the endless clamour for interviews at the close of play.

Ours is an ephemeral business and broadcasters are quickly forgotten, but Alan McGilvray's reputation deserves to live on.

When talk turns to the commentary box for Test matches in England, the legendary Brian Johnston sense of humour is never far away. The day 'Johnners' pulled his cake trick on Alan McGilvray is one of the more famous Johnston stunts. Here is McGilvray's version from The Game Is Not The Same.

Mac on his last tour of England, Edgbaston 1985. Perhaps it was only on this last tour that he fully realised how popular he was with British listeners. Patrick Eagar

ALAN McGILVRAY

'Johnners', as he is known to just about everybody, looked upon his commentary as an entertainment first and an information service second. A brilliant personality, he always stood out in a crowd. From the two-tone brown and white shoes that adorned his feet to the garish yellow and orange of his MCC tie, Johnners played the role of the social English gentleman to a tee.

He always had a joke, was always full of laughter and high spirits. For a couple of generations he was the *bon vivant* of the commentary box, a broadcaster who could talk his way through a couple of hours' break in play with articulate tales of matches past, days at the theatre, horse riding in the country—it didn't seem to matter. Johnners was in the business of keeping people entertained and that he did brilliantly, in the box and outside it.

He had an enormous following, which he played to unashamedly. He would occasionally start the day by telling his audience how ghastly he felt. I recall on one occasion he went into a sorrowful tale about how he had run out of toothpaste and couldn't brush his teeth that morning. Next day toothpaste arrived in the broadcasting box by the bucketful.

Brian got on the air next morning to thank all the ladies who sent the toothpaste. 'But I seem to have lost my toothbrush,' he complained. 'I'm afraid the toothpaste isn't much good to me without a toothbrush.' Next day a load of toothbrushes arrived from all over the country.

Johnston played to that sort of audience. He received gifts almost every day. Ladies would send him cake, fruit, sweets. Some days the box would be like a bazaar. And Brian would always acknowledge the gifts over the air, and in that way develop a personal touch in his commentaries that won him many fans.

The box was never dull when Brian Johnston was in residence. He loved to take me down a peg or two with practical jokes. His favourite was the cake trick. I had done my stint on air and was well out of the way at the other end of the commentary box, still with the headphones on listening to the commentary and with a microphone in front of me.

Johnners offered me some of the chocolate cake which had arrived in vast quantities that day. He waited until my mouth was full, and said on air: 'Now we'll ask Alan McGilvray what he thinks about that.'

There was nothing I could do but spit the cake into my hand and answer the question. Nobody heard my answer of course, because the whole commentary team was in uproar and Brian was explaining in explicit detail to the radio audience at large how I had been caught and mortally embarrassed.

I don't know how, but he actually caught me twice like that on successive tours.

That sort of bubbling good humour was Johnston's forte. He kept the commentary box a happy, frothy place, and endeared himself to millions of listeners with his infectious good humour. Cricket, to Johnston, could never be so serious that you couldn't find a good belly laugh in it. It was to be enjoyed, he reasoned, and that was the way he conveyed it to his listeners.

Peter Baxter's reference to Arthur Gilligan touches on the great partnership of McGilvray's early days in commentary ... a partnership that set many of the standards by which he operated through the rest of his career. Victor Richardson and Arthur Gilligan, two former Test cricket high achievers from their respective countries, were a double act that captured the Australian imagination of the time. The following extract is from The Game Is Not The Same . . .

Victor Richardson was a king of South Australian sport, a significant influence in a mighty era of Australian cricket, and a master pioneer broadcaster. Arthur Gilligan was a natural foil for him. He was the epitome of the English gentleman. Quiet, considerate, polite and exceedingly proper, he exuded a warmth that glowed. He didn't have the same direct, forthright manner that was Richardson's hallmark. His character was more mellow, his manner full of reason and understanding. He had a quiet assurance about him and an enormous presence. His knowledge of cricket, and his ability to encapsulate it and express it, were extraordinary.

'Johnners' was in the business of keeping people entertained and he did that brilliantly, in the box and outside it. Patrick Eagar

The two personalities complemented each other splendidly. Their balance was very much part of their success. Arthur was as thoroughly English as Vic was Australian.

My passion for cricket had been born at the Sydney Cricket Ground in 1924 when Arthur Gilligan captained England against Herbie Collins' Australian side. I did not miss a ball of that Test, and the vision of Gilligan and Collins tossing for choice of innings is as vivid in my mind now as it was sixty-odd years ago. It was sheer magic in later years to meet and play with or against most of those men. Men like Collins, Bardsley, Ponsford, Taylor, Richardson, Kellaway, Hendry, Gregory, Oldfield and Mailey. Great men.

But there was something special about the day in Melbourne in 1947 when Arthur Gilligan made his way to the broadcasting box for the third Test between Bradman's team and Hammond's team. He had held in my mind the aura that schoolboys so often associate with their sporting heroes, and to broadcast with him was a considerable event in my life.

Rarely does the reality conform with the images built from schoolboy idolatry. But in Gilligan's case, the quality of the man exceeded anything my mind could have imagined. We broadcast twenty-five England–Australia Tests together, and built a bond in our commentary team that must have come across in the descriptions. Arthur, Vic and I were fortunate that our wives— Penny Gilligan, Peg Richardson and my own late wife, Gwen— became such firm friends as well. It was a special bond that only cricket, as the catalyst, could provide.

Arthur was probably the inspiration for the friendliness that existed between us. He insisted we were a team. Whatever we did, we did as a unit. Examples of his kindliness were legion. He once organised the Sydney Cricket Ground Trust to erect a tent on the SCG no 2 oval and play host to the blind and partially blind of the two World Wars. He knew there was a small army of people, whose sight had failed them for one reason or another and for whom our radio descriptions were the only way their love of cricket could be satisfied.

Arthur organised two shifts. The World War I veterans on one day, the World War II veterans on another. He appealed over the air for people with cars to pick them up, bring them to the ground, and return them home. He organised extensive hospitality from the SCG Trust, and rounded up players from both sides to present themselves when they were not involved in the play to rub shoulders with the blind people. When Keith Miller, Ray Lindwall and Denis Compton turned up, there was pandemonium. Quite a few blind men staggered out of the SCG on those days very happy, and very obviously so.

Gilligan had had a fairly tough war. He was heavily involved administratively with the Royal Air Force in defending Britain through the darkest days of the German Luftwaffe's onslaught. He had an abiding respect for those who had fought, and those who had suffered.

It was a common event through that tour of 1946–47 for Arthur to round up Vic and myself around 8.30 in the morning and take us off to a veterans' hospital. In the immediate postwar years there were some very sick and sorry boys in those hospitals, and their delight in having Vic and Arthur visit them had to be seen to be

Arthur Gilligan—polite and proper, warm and reasonable—the perfect commentary foil for Vic Richardson.

believed. They obviously identified with them very closely through the radio cricket descriptions.

Arthur's insistence on this type of community involvement was very much part of his nature, and won him enormous respect with the Australian public at large. At home he was no different. On my first visit to England in 1948 I spent a lovely evening at his home in Sussex.

I was fascinated by the letterbox. Arthur had a family of finches nesting in it. He nurtured those finches as if they were part of the family. The postman was politely asked not to use the letterbox while the finches were in residence, and had to make a considerable trek up the drive to deliver the letters by hand to the front door. So simple a kindness touched me to the extent that I tried to repeat the procedure in my own garden back in Sydney. Unfortunately I could not get the birds to co-operate.

Arthur was not without his impish touches. There was one occasion when Vic Richardson tied himself in knots trying to describe an over from Ernie Toshack to Cyril Washbrook. It came out 'Toshbrook to Washack'. Arthur took up the challenge with a Spoonerism or two of his own. Then came the telegrams by the thousands. We had sharvellous mots that produced bine foundaries, we had exquisite fatsmen whose strokes were too good for the bieldsmen. We had Bradser carving up Bedman. On and on they went.

The listening public saw it as some sort of contest. Eventually the Post Office came to us and asked us to call a halt. Much as they wanted the business, the decoding required to make any sense of the telegrams was taking up too much of their time. Things were grinding to a halt. Vic and Arthur declared a truce, and we called 'enough' to the wild imaginings of our public.

Many commentators of real quality have graced the airwaves since cricket became a popular vehicle for serving sport to the masses, but none could match the particular place that Victor Richardson and Arthur Gilligan will always hold in the history of sport on radio.

A MATTER OF
DETAIL

by *Richie Benaud*

Richie Benaud captained Australia with great flair between 1958 and 1963. A very successful all-rounder, he held the Australian Test wicket-taking record for many years. In more recent times he has become perhaps the world's most respected cricket commentator on television.

RICHIE BENAUD

There are some of us whose cricket memories didn't begin with the television screen, it was the written and the spoken word which started us on our way in cricket. In 1936–37 during the sensational Ashes series in Australia I listened to the ABC Radio broadcasts in Jugiong; the sound came from the giant Kriesler radio in the corner of the room and Mel Morris's deep baritone was one of the voices relayed from the Corowa station. A few years later Alan McGilvray, having played for and captained the NSW Sheffield Shield team, moved into the area of cricket radio broadcasting and made it his own.

I never heard a better cricket broadcaster, though with all such judgments it is a matter of preference. I preferred, and still do, the concise factual broadcaster who knows the game and is able to add all the necessary information throughout the day so that anyone switching on their radio in a car, alongside the ironing-board or huddled beneath the bedclothes late at night, is given the complete picture of what is happening on the field.

With McGilvray it wasn't just the straightforward story he told because he also had the gift of colourful presentation, but his first job—duty was his phrase—was to provide the details before he started thinking about the flowery bits. Although fiercely Australian, he was also completely unbiased in his work and in his opinions offered to the listening public.

There have been other fine broadcasters, John Arlott was one,

Richie Benaud looking for a six in 1954. The great all-rounder laboured in his early years, relying heavily on his batting to support his progress. His cricket gained strength the moment he was appointed captain, and he is credited with abruptly bringing a fresh, positive approach to the game.

Charles Fortune the South African another, and there have been those who have aspired to copy them with varying degrees of success.

Alan formed excellent partnerships with former England captain Arthur Gilligan, and Vic Richardson the former Australian captain and splendid all-round sportsman who played for South Australia in the 1930s and then, in later years, he teamed up with Lindsay Hassett who also captained Australia as well as Victoria. Those combinations were to the benefit of all the people who turned on their radios to listen to the cricket and I always thought the greatest thing about Alan's commentary was that he welcomed them and took pleasure in keeping them enthralled as well as informed.

It's not always easy to work in tandem on a sports broadcast, but the secret of those mentioned was that they took the listeners into their confidence and took themselves to where the listeners were. There was nothing detached about it, the whole thing quickly became a happy family atmosphere and was greatly appreciated by the recipients. The other aspect was that McGilvray, Gilligan, Richardson and Hassett were equals both in an understanding of the game and, just as important, in understanding cricket followers.

They were able to do this because they had an unrivalled knowledge of the game and an ability to communicate that knowledge to every walk of life without, even for an instant, talking down to one listener.

I retired from the first-class game in 1964, having started my playing career in the NSW vs Queensland match at the SCG in the New Year match of 1949 where Alan broadcast a NSW victory. I can't remember him missing a game until I retired in 1964, nor then until his own retirement in 1985. I was one of many cricketers who knew the game had been enriched by his special talents.

Alan McGilvray made no secret of his regard for the influence Richie Benaud had on giving impetus to the game in his term as captain. He regarded Benaud, along with Ian Chappell and Don Bradman, as the most effective Australian captains of his experience. McGilvray wrote of Benaud thus in Captains Of The Game . . .

ALAN McGILVRAY

I first met Richie Benaud, so he tells me, at the old Cumberland Oval in Parramatta back in the 1930s, when Richie was all of six years of age. Even then the young Benaud was something of a devotee, following his father Lou as he trundled his leg-breaks quite successfully around the grounds of Sydney district cricket.

I batted a few times against Lou Benaud, and knew him as one of the real tradesman bowlers of Sydney cricket. He worked long and hard for his successes, as any slow bowler must, and to Australian cricket's great benefit the trait was handed down to his eldest son, Richie.

Benaud's captaincy of the Australian team was one of those appointments that had a ring of destiny about it, as if his whole cricketing life had been ordained for that one moment in time. Benaud took a long time to make it as a first class cricketer. He laboured through his early years, relying heavily on his batting to support his progress, and in retrospect benefited by more perseverance from selectors than would ever be contemplated today.

Yet his cricket gained new heights the moment he was appointed captain, and his relatively unexpected choice in that role in the late 1950s actually changed the face of cricket. It was an inspired choice. Benaud, more than any other captain before him, recognised that the game had to 'go modern'. He lifted its pace, imbued it with a new, outgoing enthusiasm, and opened it up to the public with an enlightened flair for public relations that was without precedent. And all of this came at a time when the game badly needed a shot in the arm if it was to maintain public support. Benaud gave it that, ushering in a period of successes and prosperity to match any in the game.

On the question of commentary, McGilvray also admired the Benaud way, which in another field mirrored the same sort of standard he had set for himself. Again the extract is from Captains Of The Game.

These days I admire Benaud above all others as a television commentator on cricket. It is significant to me that he does not get involved in some of the trite baiting that seems to go on between commentators who were once rivals on the cricket field. When something is put to him in quest of a 'bite', he simply remains silent. His concentration thus stays with the job in hand, and his commentaries are reasoned, full of insight and experience, and sufficiently concise and understated as not to grate on the listener.

He handles his work as a commentator with all the aplomb he once showed as a captain. And the lesson of history will always be that he was one of the game's more enlightened and influential leaders.

Richie Benaud on duty as a television commentator in England. Mac felt Benaud is without peer in this role.

THE MEDIA CLUB
by Phil Wilkins

Phil Wilkins took over as senior cricket writer for the
Sydney Morning Herald *in 1966, and through a distin-*
guished career has covered the game all over the globe.
He worked for many years with Bill O'Reilly, and
through associations with McGilvray, O'Reilly, Lindsay
Hassett et al, was able to soak up, tour after tour, the
character of a great cricket era.

PHIL WILKINS

What a trap for young players. Every night on tour in Australia, the
ceremony was the same. Cricket over for the day, work finished, commitments attended to, the two of them would adjourn to the motel
room before dinner and crack a bottle of Scotch . . . Alan McGilvray
and Lindsay Hassett. And if it wasn't two of them, there were three
or four or five with Jack Fingleton, Bill O'Reilly and Keith Miller
joining the club to keep the arguments humming and the stories, tall
and true, spinning and the firewater tumbling.

They called him 'McGilvers' in keeping with the English tradition, just as it was 'Johnners' with Brian Johnston, of the BBC. But
to most of us he was just Mac.

He was a man of strong opinion, never mealy-mouthed, never
one to shilly-shally. He could be prickly, direct, one not to tolerate
fools, but he made the *Sydney Morning Herald*'s new man feel
welcome. As a long-time colleague of the famous Tom Goodman—
Arthur Mailey said he was the most appropriately named man he ever
knew—Mac must have looked at the *Herald*'s young buck with
serious reservations. What he thought, he kept to himself.

It was 1967–68, the summer of the Nawab of Pataudi's Indians
in Australia, and if they could not bat as a world class combination,
they certainly paraded a spin bowling trio in Erapalli Prasanna,
Bhagwat Chandrasekhar and Bishan Singh Bedi to rank with any in
the history of the game, a trio who floated and weaved mysteries
through the air and off the pitch like the unlikeliest spiders.

One of the strange quirks of the cricket media game is that although newspaper and radio men are invariably situated side by side up behind the arm in the pavilion, rarely are they aware of the other's work so that when Mac went into his broadcasting box, his words carried to all points of the compass, transmitted all around the world, yet they fell on deaf ears as far as the journalists next door were concerned, locked away in their own enclosure, in their own little world, ignorant of his impressions.

But to a schoolboy, Alan McGilvray brought cricket to his home, to his paddock, to his planet, the voice who introduced by word picture, who made immortal in his mind's eye, the most important memory hall of all, the images of players like Bill O'Reilly, Keith Miller, Neil Harvey, Don Bradman, Ray Lindwall and George Tribe, his words beaming into the little mining village of Drake, a place of barely 100 people up on the eastern fall of the Great Divide, to a cow-pat covered field called Wattle Flat in the bend of an arm of Plumbago Creek, where cricket came to have a meaning with a rigid, one-piece bat cut from a slab of old willow, where a hereford cattle station owner from Cheviot Hills named Rod Ramsay and the local post master named Pat Lawrence became heroes with their six-hitting into the creek against Tabulam, Bonalbo and Mallanganee.

Mac called it before the kid was born at the start of the war. So it was with gratitude that after eventually playing under the captaincy of the ageless phenomenon, the NSW cricketer-baseballer, Ken Gulliver, at Mosman club, the country boy came to meet the bespectacled stranger with the voice as familiar as that of his father.

On first acquaintance, he was very formal, very proper, as you would expect of an ABC man, somewhat stiff and straight-laced, with tie and suit, as you would think of a man whose words carried around the globe or at least to all the red portions on the map of the British Empire.

But time quickly broke down any barrier of age or qualification. Mac told it how he saw it, on air or off it. But he was generous to the new man. During that first Adelaide Test, at the old Travelodge where the team always stayed opposite the broad parkland with its avenues of pink-flowering white cedars and hay-gold grass belt, the novice accepted an invitation to join Mac and his elfin mate Hassett for a drink, long after they had started, pool-side in the warm, still evening.

When they decided enough was enough, he offered to drive Lindsay back to his pub.

'Turn right,' came the terse order. A quarter of an hour later with the car heading out into the Mount Lofty Ranges, the voice snapped: 'Where do you think you're going?'

'You said turn right.'

'You're going in the wrong direction. It's back the other way.'

Half an hour later, we got Lindsay home. Mac explained later: 'He's a leprechaun. He will have his little joke.'

The scotches with Mac and Lindsay went on for years until the radio partnership ended and Lindsay disappeared into retirement to Batemans Bay, taking his pipe with him. When the little Victorian and Australian Test captain passed away in 1993, at 79, a grieving Mac said of his crony: 'He was the best I worked with as a team.' Then the objective side of the commentator emerged: 'He was a good leader—didn't show much imagination, but he was always planning something, cunning little bugger.'

Time passed and Bob Simpson, recalled to the Test captaincy after a decade out of the limelight although still involved in club cricket with Western Suburbs, led the Australian team to the West Indies. It was 1978 and World Series Cricket was in full swing.

Lindsay Hassett and Mac together as commentators. Mac felt a great rapport with Hassett and believed the teamwork they developed over the years was one of the highlights of his working life.

Simpson led a talented team of novices away on the most gruelling of tours.

The side reached Guyana on the South American mainland and communications were next to impossible as electrical failures kept recurring, eight or nine hours at a time. The Demerara rum, cut and crushed from the local sugar cane, was the only solace in times of such frustration.

It was hot and humid and there was no electricity or running water and we gathered on the sixth floor of the Pegasus Hotel. It was a rest day and the lifts were grounded so we settled in for a long session. Mac not only had acute communication difficulties, he also had a back condition which was causing him untold agony. He lay on his bed while we drank around him. Peering around the door emerged a blue and white-aproned housemaid. Mac explained his problem. Lo, this wonder woman was not simply a housemaid, she was also an angel with Florence Nightingale hands. By mid-afternoon, Mac was back on his feet and the old gleam was back in his eye. But that did not restore the electricity.

It was later in the West Indies that Mac descended from the press box at the Maraval Hills end of Port-of-Spain's Queen's Park Oval intending to cross the ground to have lunch in the Members' Pavilion. He found three black, burly and very ugly spectators barring his path.

'You got money, white dog?' enquired their spokesman.

'I'm going to have my lunch, my good man,' spluttered Mac with disbelief. 'Now, out of my way.' And he stepped around the three desperadoes and enjoyed his lunch, relating the incident with passion to suitably impressed journalists, barely able to contain their mirth at the impertinence of the miscreants and the indignation of their intended victim.

Forever after, the doyen was referred to as 'White God' by his Australian colleagues.

The role of the 'expert comment' man in cricket broadcasting was, Alan McGilvray always contended, vital to the 'life' of the commentary. It provided shade and subtlety. Teamwork in the commentary box was the soul of the business. McGilvray had many respected co-commentators, but as Phil Wilkins has recalled, he struck a special empathy with Lindsay Hassett.

The extract from Captains Of The Game *leaves little doubt as to where Hassett stood in the McGilvray estimation . . .*

ALAN McGILVRAY

As both a captain and a commentator, Lindsay Hassett was a team man. The years I spent with him in commentary boxes around the nation left me in no doubt of that. He had a knowledge and an understanding of cricket that few could match, yet there was an earthy perspective to all he said and did that made sure the game, first and foremost, was always just that ... a game. It was all fun to Lindsay, and it came through as we worked together for so many years, feeding lines and thoughts to each other as if our minds were somehow computer-linked. He used to drive me mad with his incessant pipe-smoking—sometimes I thought he smoked merely matches, so much time did he spend lighting his pipe—but it was a small price to pay for that innate good humour that made him such splendid company.

As a captain Hassett is not remembered as one of the greats, although his win–loss record is second only to Bradman's among postwar captains. He captained Australia 24 times for 14 wins, compared to Bradman's 15 wins from 24 Tests. Considering Bradman had the inestimable advantage of Bradman himself, that was a pretty good record. Yet you never hear Hassett mentioned in the same breath as Woodfull or Ryder, who had gone before, or Benaud or Chappell who followed. Hassett's place in the history of captaincy suffered on a couple of counts. First of all, he was the skipper who followed Bradman, and that was a bit akin to being the next playwright after Shakespeare.

Bradman had commanded the stage as none before him, not just for the mastery of his batting but also for the sheer presence of his place in cricket history. He had been around a long time thanks to the intervention of the war, and was revered at the time of his retirement by a generation of young devotees who, as children, had marvelled at his magic. He was also a shrewd, calculating captain who had been richly successful. As such he was an institution, and Hassett knew that following him would bring comparisons that would always leave him in his shadow.

The other factor to count against Hassett was the long wait

for the job. Hassett had come into first class cricket as a twenty-year-old in 1933, made the Test side as a dashing twenty-four-year-old in 1938, and then assumed the Test captaincy in 1949 at thirty-six. Most of his Test cricket thus was played well into his thirties. Hassett had captained the Australian Services team through World War II and was noted as a marvellous stroke player, with all the quicksilver traits in speed of foot, eye and hand that seem to be the preserve of smaller men. In his later years he reshaped his game to the needs of his team and the captaincy. He played more conservatively and, perhaps because he feared advancing years, would not allow himself some of the luxuries that the sharp reflexes of pre-war years encouraged.

The result was a more conservative batsman, conscious always of the need to put backbone in an innings, even if it took time. I believe he may have come to regret that shift in emphasis, despite the fact he was highly successful, averaging better than 46 runs per innings through his 43 Tests. I know that many times through our period as a commentary team when he had torn strips off somebody who had bogged down at the crease, he would admonish himself. 'Thank goodness,' he would say, 'there was nobody like me up here when I was down there'. It made the point, with the benefit of hindsight, that he looked back on his batting of latter years with less than great delight.

A FOND FAREWELL

by Max Walker

Max Walker was a well-performed Test fast-bowler in the mid 1970s who has since achieved distinction as a commentator, television presenter, author and raconteur. His beginnings in the world of media involved some valued lessons from Alan McGilvray, and he was on hand for an emotional SCG farewell.

MAX WALKER

After my retirement as a player I made my debut as a cricket commentator at Kardinia Park, Geelong, in January 1982. Drew Morphett and I covered the match between Victoria and South Australia for ABC TV from 10.59 am on day one till 6.00 pm at the end of day four! The wicket was fast and hundreds of runs were scored between many slow moments ... it was difficult at times describing grass growing, seagulls landing, and the odd stray dog trespassing on to the field at fine leg.

At the end of the day Drew was asked how the 'big fella' had performed? 'This bloke's unreal,' Drew replied. 'He can talk under water with a mouth full of marbles!' That was the beginning.

Several weeks later I found myself progressing to calling a one-day international between Australia and the West Indies in front of a huge crowd at the MCG. On that occasion I shared the microphone with the doyen of Australian radio commentators, Alan McGilvray. It was a more nerve-wracking experience than bowling my first inswinger in my debut Test. I had earlier met Mac during the 1973 tour to the West Indies. He was such an easy man to warm to ... articulate, humorous and always the perfect host. He loved to share a yarn or two over a scotch or dinner with cricket people.

A decade later, before going on air, my friend gave me some invaluable advice. 'Son,' he said, 'if you imagine you are talking to a blind man when you're describing the game ... satisfy his needs and you'll do alright.' Call it colour radio. Mac was brilliant at creating indelible word pictures about the game he passionately loved—images that will linger for a lifetime.

I have been lucky enough to enjoy the company of three of the game's finest voices, each a magnificent communicator. On two tours of England it was a wonderfully enriching experience to make friends with the gravel-voiced historian and wine expert John Arlott. While visiting South Africa it was a pleasure to meet Charles Fortune, a man whom I listened to as a boy for many a long hour. But more than any it was the silky smooth voice of Alan McGilvray that lit the fire in my belly that made me want to become a Test cricketer . . . to dream night after night of pulling on a green baggy cap.

I'll never forget those magnificent sound waves that crackled and bounced from one side of the world to the other instantaneously describing the events through the headphones of my home-made crystal set. Each of these gentlemen had a burning passion for the greatest game of all, based on a lifetime involvement. They also had the ability to put into words a rare insight into proceedings, no matter what the predicament. They were all commonsense and unflappable composure. Because of their talents it would appear to listeners that there are rarely problems, but let me share an occasion or two where things didn't quite work out to plan. In fact the Australia v West Indies limited-overs match at the MCG in 1982 was just the beginning of several interesting situations.

The ABC radio commentator's box in those days was not the most aesthetically pleasing piece of architecture at the Melbourne Cricket Ground. Located at the back of the cigar smokers' stand (MCG members) on the top level it resembled a crude chook house—split level over two seats approximately two metres by three metres with a corrugated iron roof but without the wire mesh front. Sliding glass windows represented the only significant difference.

On that unforgettable day the temperature hovered around 45 degrees Celsius. It was very, very hot! In order to occupy my position at the microphone as expert comments man, I had to climb bodily over the shoulders of Mac and our ever reliable master of statistics, Jack Cameron. With a nickname like Tanglefoot, standing 6 ft 4 ins tall and sending the rev counter on the scales racing towards 17 stone I was never going to achieve my objective without incident. Even the doorway into the confined space presented a struggle—it sloped across the top from right to left about 5 ft to 3 ft 6 ins.

I felt like a dog entering his kennel. Batting hero of the 1960s

In the front row, left to right: veteran scorer Jack Cameron, Mac, Johnny Moyes and Bob Richardson. Straight behind Mac is the Victorian Sporting Supervisor Ken Dakin, who had the habit of interrupting commentators from that position by tapping them on the shoulder. He only tried it once with Mac. Many years later Cameron and Mac were stomped on by a tanglefooted Max Walker in the commentary box.

Norman O'Neill had just completed his hour long stint. As he stood up it was clear to see not a stitch of his clothing was dry. He could not have perspired that much had he scored a century. My leading knee-cap clipped dear old Mac smack bang on the back of his head . . . the pair of binoculars he was holding went close to shattering his reading glasses and the veteran student of the game almost swallowed the cigarette he was enjoying. I knew I was in trouble when he started coughing with an unhealthy barking sound. Step number two got me into more strife. Remember there were no Unisys computers spitting out green figures on a backlit screen in those days. Jack either stored them in his head or in several shoe boxes that he never let out of his sight (50 years of accumulated averages, aggregates and match results painstakingly handwritten onto small cards). As my size eleven shoe landed on the lid of his priceless shoe box, our scorer let out an almighty shout of disbelief. While his words echoed around the members' stand, cards spewed out onto the rows of spectators. Two out of two—and the new boy still had a pace to go.

There are no commercial breaks on the ABC. The broadcast box was in a state of upheaval. Mac and Jack eyeballed the intruder with looks that could send a keen mind blank. The two technicians were trying desperately to suppress uncontrollable bouts of laughter. By the time I finally sank into my seat my nerves were shot, but both forgave me in a big hurry and nursed me though the next hour together. Somehow it was difficult not to think about who called the first hour—Norm O'Neill. Now Norm is the sort of bloke who enjoys a drink *even* on a cold day. The pair of headphones had filled like cups with stale sweat 'n' beer. As I exercised my jaw, Norm's stay in the box trickled down my neck and lingered longer than any after shave. My new Pierre Cardin blazer especially obtained for the occasion, looked as if it had been swimming in it! Bad luck about the under armpit odour—even Aerogard wouldn't have worked in these conditions!

There also have been some very serious and emotional moments. During the fifth Test between Australia and the West Indies in Sydney in 1985, Alan McGilvray was calling his 219th Test—his last in Australia. During the fourth day's play we witnessed the emotional departure of one of the game's greatest ambassadors, Clive Lloyd. The big cat snaked his way from the ground, dragging the 3 lb 5 oz piece of willow in his shadow, lingering as if to slowly soak up the standing ovation afforded him for his marvellous contribution to the game of cricket.

At tea-time only two West Indies wickets remained intact. This would be a memorable victory for Allan Border and certainly this session would be Mac's last. Coincidence had Max Walker rostered to share the time slot.

Alan Marks, the executive producer for ABC cricket, had asked Mac if he would be in the box five minutes early to give some special comments. The real reason was to hear a special taped tribute to Alan from the then Prime Minister, Bob Hawke. This had to be taped because no-one could pre-determine the conclusion of the Test match or Alan's last shift on air. Mac settled into his chair then he heard his name come over the public address system. There was a mix-up. The high-tech electronic scoreboard had begun to broadcast the PM's tribute for all to hear—45 seconds earlier than ABC Radio. Once Mac had recognised the voice he took off his headphones and pulled the sliding glass windows open in order to hear more. Then we had drama as Alan Marks asked Mac to close the windows and trust him. Firstly he refused. He eventually agreed only when he heard that same voice come through his head-set.

What Bob Hawke had to say obviously moved the veteran commentator. Alan looked at me and said quietly: 'My goodness gracious me, what have I done to deserve this? I'm just a cricket commentator. I do my job like everybody else!' Then, as the game was due to get under way for the final session of play, the diamond-vision screen of the huge electronic scoreboard came to life in a kaleidoscope of colour with the words 'Thanks Mac, you are the greatest' etched into the 40 000 light globes that constitute the screen.

Simultaneously 25 000 stood to a man and turned away from the game with eyes cast high to Alan McGilvray in the commentary box at the rear of the Sir Donald Bradman stand. Hands above their heads they gave the man who belonged to the voice, who so many people had loved and respected for almost 50 years, a thunderous, standing ovation. Two balls had been bowled in the middle as we both stood before the crowd. Mac lifted his hands just as royalty would. Here was a moment very special in Australian sport.

I thought to myself: 'Might as well go out in sympathy with him,' so I stood up. The old bloke was choked with emotion. At this stage there was a steady stream of tears rolling down, past the purple nose of the silver-haired legend. Several splashed on the exercise book below. Back went the sliding glass window again . . . in came a huge lens mounted on a television camera. This time I asked myself a question, 'Gee Maxie, you want to look good on the ABC News tonight . . . get that rib cage up where it ought to be!' So I sucked in one almighty great breath . . . and hung on! Mac might have been crying but I was in real pain and my face too was going purple. How long can a mere mortal hold his breath for?

Then like the true professional, Mac sat down, regained his composure, thanked several people for their contribution to his career as a communicator, and called the remaining deliveries of the over.

Alan McGilvray wasn't just another commentator. For almost half a century, from the 1938 synthetic Test match broadcasts, he was the undisputed voice of cricket in Australia. He ended his innings with grace a few minutes later at the end of the second over when he asked Alan Marks: 'Is it possible to have another commentator in the commentary booth please? I would now like to leave.' The old bloke just stood up, turned and immediately walked away from Test cricket in Australia. Then, with the Master's chair momentarily vacant, I was left with three options, realising that the lump formerly in my throat was now somewhere up near my ears and the atmosphere in the enclosed booth was very emotional . . . as thick as a London fog.

Firstly, I could commence a ball-by-ball commentary, something I hadn't attempted in the past; secondly I could give my expert opinion on the last 10 or so deliveries bowled, none of which I'd taken much notice of; or finally, I could put in a few well-earned words of praise. I opted for the latter.

You couldn't let a man with a perspective of calling 219 Test matches and almost 50 years just get up and disappear through the rear door. I spoke from the heart about laying on the floor of the

Max Walker in action. A courageous bowler who several times won Tests for Australia when the odds were stacked against it. Mac was impressed by his positive approach and single-minded, never-say-die dedication to the Australian cause.

Empire Hotel in Hobart with the ABC cricket book open to the score-board pages, HB pencil in hand. Later that night, well after stumps, it would have been easy for Clive Lloyd in defeat to use the security of the dressing room to hide his emotion and for Mac to attend a special guests only function in retirement. But no, these two great ambassadors for the game predictably decided to mingle with their public—admirers and friends. Whilst ever someone wanted to shout Mac a scotch and Clive a rum the pair held court recounting anecdote after anecdote, seated at the corner of the SCG's famous long room bar. It was a rare privilege to be one of the crowd. Play finished around midnight. Unforgettable!

Yes, there's no doubt Mac was a class act, a true gentleman in the gentleman's game. He leaves cricket lovers with a rich tapestry of his time at the crease. He probably never realised how many lives he touched. Thanks Mac. You really were the greatest.

As an expert commentator, Max Walker shared Alan McGilvray's last broadcast in Australia, at the final West Indies Test of 1984–85. As a cricketer he had won McGilvray's admiration years before as a player of great courage.

McGilvray paints the picture in this extract from The Game Is Not The Same . . .

ALAN McGILVRAY

Cricketers through the ages have fallen into several well-defined categories. There are those who are richly talented and use that talent well. They are extremely few. There are many more who are very talented, and rely on that talent alone to achieve their success. They usually achieve moderately, and never reach their full potential. There are those who have little talent but an enormous capacity for work, who achieve a great deal more than the more talented people they overtake.

In the middle there is a large group whose talent is moderate, but who, by their iron wills, their big hearts and their determination to succeed, make the most of every ounce of talent they possess. These are real achievers, the ultimate competitors on whom most great teams are built.

Max Walker was such a competitor. Max has an outlook on life that reflects the power of positive thinking. In my last years as a Test match broadcaster I had the pleasure to work with him. He introduced to ABC broadcasts the brightness and good humour that were his trademark when he was an Australian fast-bowler. He was beside me, in fact, for my last stint at the Test match microphone in Sydney at the end of the West Indies–Australia series of 1984–85. He had to rescue me at the end when a speech of farewell by the Australian Prime Minister, Bob Hawke, was broadcast over the public address system and somewhat undermined my composure.

As a cricketer, Max seemed to do most things wrong. Wrong as far as text books go anyway. He had an awkward bowling action that unwound like a windmill at the end. It earned him the nickname 'Tanglefoot', later abbreviated to 'Tangles', very early in his career.

Walker burst on to the Test match scene against Pakistan in 1973 and cleaned them up in Sydney in only his second Test. Dennis Lillee had injured his back and was bowling under great duress. Tangles slipped into the breach, grabbing 6–15 in Pakistan's second innings. He took five wickets for three runs off his last 30 deliveries and Pakistan were all out for 106 when they had only needed 159 to win the game. They were the sort of odds on which he seemed to thrive. He bowled on his courage.

When Ian Chappell's team reached the West Indies in 1973 that courage was to be fully tested. The Australian team was extremely well equipped in the pace department when they started off. Dennis Lillee and Bob Massie had put England to the sword the previous year, and Walker was merely their backup. In the event Lillee and Massie broke down and it was left to Walker to pick up the pieces. Lillee played only in the first Test before the stress fractures in his back that very nearly ended his career put him out of business. Massie did not play a Test at all.

Walker was confronted with some hot batting talent, uninviting pitches, and a considerable lack of experience as a front-line new ball bowler. To Max, they were mere challenges. He finished the series with 27 wickets, three times took five wickets in an innings, and was the principal factor in a 2–0 series win which reflected great credit on an improvised Australian team.

It also reflected great credit on the skipper Ian Chappell, who was at his absolute best in this series in moulding a relatively unlikely bunch into a winning outfit. It was a tour in which skilful improvisation won the day. He managed to drag the best out of everybody.

By the fourth Test in Guyana, Australia held a shaky 1–0 lead, but were battling injuries and illness and they knew they would need to perform well to stay in front. On the morning that match started I was waiting for a cab to the ground. Max Walker arrived in the hotel foyer at the same time. He was barefoot, and walking on his tip toes. The backs of his legs were a mess. Blood vessels had burst. He was black and blue and generally in a dreadful state. It looked as if it would be impossible to get a boot on, let alone bowl in a Test match.

'Max,' I said. 'You can't possibly play in that condition. You'll do yourself terrible damage.' His reply was the story of the tour. 'Somebody has to do it, mate,' he said.

Australia lost the toss and were in the field that morning. Walker bowled 38 overs in the first innings, his feet packed in foam rubber, then another 25 in the second, and finished with five wickets for the match. That performance typified the outlook of that side. They would do anything for Chappell and they would leave no stone unturned to win. Walker's effort was true grit. He could hardly walk, let alone run, yet he shut the pain from his mind and bowled as well as it was possible for him to do.

MAN OF
INFLUENCE
by Dick Tucker

Dick Tucker was cricket writer for the Sydney Daily
Mirror *through three decades. His penchant for stunning
back page stories found an often fruitful trigger in Alan
McGilvray, with one particularly spectacular result.*

DICK TUCKER

WHEN it rains for six days there is plenty of time to let your imagination run riot, especially if you are paid to entertain as was Alan
McGilvray and his ABC crew covering the third Test between
Australia and England on Ray Illingworth's 1970–71 tour. With six
days of seemingly incessant rain through the Melbourne New Year
only the toss was possible. After two days without play it became
obvious a worthwhile Test would not be possible.

On the Friday night in the Cricketers' Bar of the Windsor Hotel,
the traditional home in those days for both teams, Mac and myself
became involved in a deep discussion about the pros and cons of
staging a seventh Test to compensate for the one that was already
ruined and more than likely rained out altogether. As the conversation
became more animated the solution became obvious—the ideal spot
was already there on the itinerary with precious little upheaval. Simply
replace the non-event return match between the tourists and Victoria
and the Victorian country outing late in January with the extra Test.
In the confines of the Windsor bar it all seemed so logical. In reality,
of course, it was verging on the preposterous to suggest the ultra-
conservative administrations of both countries would agree to such a
radical change.

The one ray of hope was that Australian Board chairman Sir
Donald Bradman was in his most receptive and affable mood. Hell,
he talked to the media at will and was even photographed in his
pyjamas, the picture being prominently displayed on the front page of
the Melbourne *Herald*. But that wasn't a consideration when

McGilvray and his main cohort, former Australian captain Lindsay Hassett, launched their seventh Test campaign the following morning.

My story appeared on the front page of the Sydney *Daily Mirror*, which had no influence on what was happening in Melbourne, while Norm Tasker of the Sydney *Sun* refused to be involved with what was no more than an apparently impossible suggestion, despite pleas from his persistent editor who was caught up by the powers of persuasion of McGilvray on the ABC. By midday rumours started circulating the old press box at the Melbourne Cricket Ground that the heavyweights of both boards were engrossed in talks with the MCC tour manager David Clark. About two hours later Bradman, the two visiting MCC officials Sir Cyril Hawker and 'Gubby' Allen, and Clark, walked into the press box and announced their decision to stage the extra Test in the suggested time frame.

I relate this story because Bradman and company were influenced by McGilvray's simple logic and his powers of persuasion, and the high regard they held for him (and of course Hassett, Bradman's most able deputy in many a struggle). Mac was compulsive listening for all levels of cricket from the Don down to the avid young supporter listening to his simulated broadcasts pre-war on a crystal set. Certainly, his closest of mates, Keith Miller, has no reservations about Mac power. In daily contact with him over the last few years Miller always proclaimed that Mac had one of the most astute and knowledgeable cricket brains in the country and would back him in discussions against anyone in the world. Doug Walters put him on a pedestal among cricket brains. When Walters first met McGilvray in Brisbane after his century in the first of 74 Tests, he felt honoured to be introduced to him—the century-making hero revering the commentator.

'I was in awe of him,' admitted Walters. 'He was cricket to me and my family. It was just tremendous to meet in person the man who had brought so much happiness to our family over the years. I listened to him from the first time I knew there was such a game as cricket. We later became regular after hours companions in his room and I feel he contributed to my success by discussing the deeds of the great men of the past when he was NSW captain and before. He didn't tell you what to do but made suggestions and explained how some of his contemporaries—the legends of the game like Stan McCabe and Bradman—played certain deliveries. But what I remember most about Mac was the confidence he instilled in me.

'When I went out to bat I felt not only I mustn't let myself down but also I couldn't disappoint him because he was such a staunch Aussie who couldn't stand being beaten, especially by the Poms. If I did fail or the team as a whole had a bad day he wasn't critical. He would look on the brighter side of things rather than dwell on the dismal aspects.'

Like most of his close associates Walters had a special anecdote to recall about McGilvray. It was during the fourth Test against the West Indies in Guyana in 1973 when Australia clinched the rubber.

'On the first evening he came to the dressing room and told our captain Ian Chappell that the pitch was perfect for the leg-spin of Terry Jenner and Kerry O'Keeffe,' said Walters. 'The result was the spinners didn't take a wicket, all of them falling to the pace men.' Walters himself picked up seven for the match. 'It just proved that Mac was fallible after all,' he added.

Rod Marsh who with Ian Chappell, Brian Taber and Walters were among McGilvray's closest player confidants also has a favourite McGilvray story concerning that Guyana Test when there was more than a hint of Black Power aggression in the crowd, especially with the West Indies tumbling.

'After stumps Mac rushed to the safety of our dressing room, flustered and angry as hell,' Marsh said. ' "Good God," he said. "One of those beggars pissed on me through the stands." In many ways Mac was an old stuff shirt, more English than the English. He reckoned he had never been demeaned so much in his life.'

Marsh also related with relish the trip home from the West Indies: 'Mac was fed up with his companions in first class so he hijacked Doug and myself into the captain's lounge of the old Qantas plane. After an hour or so a flight attendant suggested we all go back to our seats as we were half an hour out of Honolulu. We went back and stretched out and the next thing I remember is Mac tapping me on the shoulder and suggesting we resume our conversation. I spluttered that we were half an hour out of Honolulu. "I know," he answered. "We're half an hour out on the other side on the way to Sydney." Doug and I had slept through the landing and of course it was the last sleep we had until we got back home.'

Unlike Walters, Marsh was not overawed when he was first introduced to Mac. In fact, he was singularly unimpressed. 'He was just another commentator,' he said. But from that casual meeting during Marsh's 'iron gloves' debut series in 1970–71 a firm friendship was established.

'It blossomed on the tours and one of the favourite memories of my playing days was sitting down with him and talking about cricket,' Marsh recalled. 'When he criticised me on the radio he would always try to be first to tell me about it. It might have been an insurance policy in case I heard it from someone else. He would say: "I got into you today Marshie ... you were too slow getting up to the stumps," or something like that.'

Marsh's summary of Mac was straightforward: 'I never thought of him as a God-like figure, just a bloody good Australian who liked to have a drink and was fiercely loyal to Australian cricket. He was good to be around because he had been around for so long. I've never known such a loyal Australian who hated with a passion being beaten by the Poms. I couldn't believe that someone who was supposed to be impartial was so biased yet it never reflected on his commentary. In fact, he was renowned for his impartiality and that was the way he always came across.'

Brian Taber

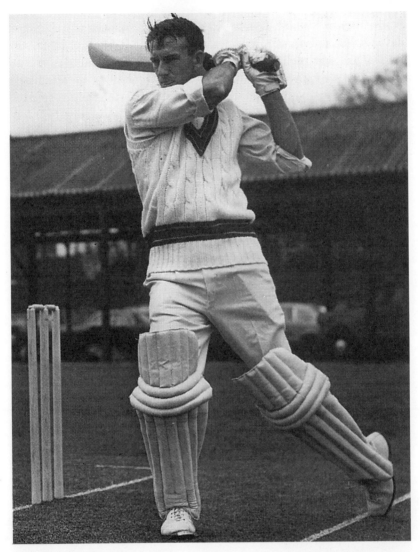

Doug Walters

Norm O'Neill reckons he was privileged to share the best of two worlds with Mac, first as a cricketer throughout his 42 Tests and then as a co-commentator with him on the ABC. Their first meeting was when Mac interviewed him as a NSW Colt.

'The next was when we shared a cab back to the team's hotel after my Test debut, in Brisbane in 1958,' said O'Neill. 'He shared the experience with me, talking over the huge difference between first-class cricket and Tests. The interest he took in me was a great buzz because he was such a legend in his own right. From then on we became pretty close. You could tell him anything. If you had a

Rod Marsh Patrick Eagar

Brian Taber, Doug Walters, Rod Marsh and Ian Chappell, pictured here, were Mac's closest player confidants in the 1970s.

problem he was always there to listen. He didn't offer a great deal of advice but would make suggestions. He was held in tremendous respect by the players.'

After he retired O'Neill ran a cricket school at the WACA in Perth and came into contact occasionally with McGilvray as a part-time commentator. Their association became more intense in 1980 when he returned to Sydney and became a regular member of the ABC team.

'Again he helped me a great deal but three aspects of our association stand out,' he said. 'Firstly there was his reaction when I interrupted him while he was calling an over; how he changed the format of ABC calling; and his tenseness when he faced up to the microphone in the mornings. In my first series with him in 1980 I chipped in with an opinion when he was doing the ball by ball. He ignored me for the rest of the day but when we went for dinner that night he said: "Do you mind if I give you a word of advice. Don't ever interrupt when the ball by ball man is talking." Strangely enough, a few

*Norm O'Neill during the 1958–59 summer. A fine attacking batsman from the late
1950s and early 1960s, he came to treasure Mac's ideas and suggestions about his
game. Later the two became extremely close mates.*

seasons later when the West Indies were out here he changed his mind
about that. In fact, he encouraged comments during an over because
the West Indies' fast bowlers were taking so damn long to complete
an over. He reckoned it gave more life to the coverage.'

Concerning McGilvray's nervousness before the start of a Test
O'Neill confessed he was most surprised. 'I wondered; if Mac shows
signs of stress maybe Bradman did before he went out to bat,' said
O'Neill, renowned for his nervousness before the start of an innings.
'Mac used to come into the box, light up a cigarette, sit down, study
the papers in front of him and not say a word for five minutes or so.
Once he started to talk though there was no sign of tension. His voice
was just clear and distinctive as always.'

Another trait O'Neill recalled was the dinner time ritual. 'As we
walked to our table he would declare: ''Alright Norm, we've talked
cricket all day we won't talk about it tonight.'' Inevitably after 10
minutes the subject would come back and we would talk cricket until
the wee small hours.'

McGilvray told O'Neill his biggest disappointment was flying
home with Keith Miller before the end of the tied Test in Brisbane in
1960 and missing out on a slice of history. 'He never left a match

after that even though it may have been pouring with rain,' he added. O'Neill was in the ABC box when McGilvray worked at his last Test at the SCG in the mid-80s. 'When it was announced on the scoreboard everyone in the Noble Stand turned towards us and clapped,' said O'Neill. 'Mac just stood there with the tears rolling down his cheeks. It was a sad and touching moment.'

As well as his affinity with the players McGilvray enjoyed an extra special rapport with two of the country's former Test umpires Col Egar and Lou Rowan. From the time the umpiring pair joined forces for the first of their 19 Tests together, the fifth Test against England at the SCG in 1963, they became a happy trinity—three men devoted to their particular skills and sharing it with each other. The first part of the tri-party agreement fell into place on the morning of the tied Test in Brisbane.

'Mac came to the umpires' room at the 'Gabba, introduced himself and suggested after the day's play we socialise,' explained Egar. 'I was surprised and delighted that a man of his standing in the game would want to meet me, and wish me luck standing in my first Test. From then on we got together after every day of the Tests and enjoyed each other's company.'

When Rowan joined the party it was again a case of instant

Captains Gary Sobers and Bill Lawry after Australia's success in the series in Australia, 1968–69. Prominent in the background is umpire Lou Rowan, who along with Col Egar developed an 'intelligence system' for his mate Mac in the commentary box.

rapport, initially between the two umpires and then with Mac. They each doffed their hat towards him in the ABC box on the second morning of the Sydney Test. 'It became a ritual for every session because we knew Mac was always first up in the commentary team,' explained Egar. 'Similarly, before the start of play each day he would drop in and wish us luck and say "don't make too many mistakes". My answer was always the same: "And the same to you." '

Of the oft-mentioned signs between the umpiring pair to which Mac became privy, Egar refrained from being explicit. 'Neither Mac nor Lou in their books explained them, so I don't think it is my place to be too specific about them,' he said. 'Suffice to say they were hand signals, a touch of the shoulder or the nose, stuff like that.'

What should have been common knowledge but what few other media men picked up on was Egar's habit before he gave a batsman out. 'I was slightly stooped as I watched the delivery but before I raised my finger I instinctively came to attention,' Egar explained. 'It was a sort of reflex action that never changed and Mac was always first to call it right. On repeated occasions I remember Mac's colleagues praising him for being so quick and decisive. That applied for other signals as well. I never heard any reports back that he had called it wrong. Mind you, it was a case of if we were wrong so was he.'

But Egar did recall one glaring communication foul-up in Sydney when Rowan was in a joking mood. He let it slip that Egar's first dismissal of the day would be his 100th in Tests. 'Unfortunately, one of McGilvray's underlings overheard the remark and eagerly reported it to his leader.' Egar explained. 'Sure enough I gave a batsman out in the first session and Mac called it as my century of dismissals. My father heard it and relayed it to me. Later I talked to Mac about it and told him it was a Rowan furphy. Mac was unimpressed and his informant got his comeuppance.'

McGilvray's censure of his informant was typical. He was intolerant of incompetence; quick to respond to any slights or injustices and fiercely protective of his privacy. Brian Taber tells the story of how Mac and Bob Simpson, captain of the side, fell out early on the South African tour of 1967. Mac promptly booked out of the team hotel for the remainder of the tour. Then Rowan remembers the story about the aspiring young umpire who had heard about Mac's special relationship with Egar and himself and had offered to supply him with his own brand of signals. 'Mac quickly sent him packing—cut him off at the knees,' said Rowan. 'He felt the young umpire was impinging on a very special liaison and understanding between close friends.'

Rowan, a policeman for 32 years, had a more understated approach about his friendship with McGilvray. 'I just treated him as an equal,' he said. 'I regarded him as a man of high intellect, fiercely honest and of enormous experience who captained NSW when it really meant something. As far as the signals were concerned, it just wasn't on with anyone else. It was something special.' Like the others Rowan had a story that showed Mac was mortal, susceptible to the odd error.

'It was during the West Indies–Queensland game in 1969,' he recalls. 'He kept on insisting that Lance Gibbs should be brought on to get the tourists out of trouble. What he forgot was that Gibbs was only on the field as a replacement.' But the story Rowan enjoyed most about Mac concerned Bradman and just how tough a school it was in those days under his regime. 'One day at the SCG Mac threw the wickets down from side on to run someone out,' Rowan said. 'Mac was tickled pink with his effort until the little bloke (Bradman) came over to him and grimaced: ''If you had missed the stumps it would have gone for four overthrows.'' '

Mention of the Don again brings back memories of the glowing tribute he paid to McGilvray on his retirement. He said: 'That one man could have a successful and honourable career at the microphone extending over 50 years is quite astonishing. It happened mainly because Alan stuck rigidly to those essential qualities of integrity and impartiality which brought him goodwill and acclamation from all cricket-playing nations.' All his cricketing mates would heartily agree. And they'd add an extra word of admiration.

One of the more important advantages which Alan McGilvray built into his commentaries, as raised by Dick Tucker, was his ability to 'read' the idiosyncrasies of the umpires. In a couple of celebrated cases, there was a special 'intelligence network' which proved a great help.
The following extract from The Game Is Not The Same *tells the story.*

ALAN McGILVRAY

One of the best accolades I ever had as a cricket commentator was the puzzled look on one of my colleagues in Brisbane after I had called a dismissal. 'Goodness Mac, you've got good eyes,' he said, shaking his head in undisguised awe. He was not the only commentator through the years who was rather astounded by my speed in picking up something on the field. I would occasionally nominate the bouncer before it was bowled, explain with certainty that the finest of nicks was the ball flicking the pad, nominate a man out before the umpire's finger was up.

Before I sound like I'm singing my own praises as some sort of eagle-eyed fountain of knowledge, I have to concede some inside information. Most of those quick assessments of what had taken place were conveyed to me, quickly and certainly, by umpires with whom I had developed a comprehensive communications system. In the days of Col Egar and Lou Rowan, undoubtedly the best umpires I ever saw, as many as twenty signals were in operation. They kept me fully informed, quickly and accurately, on every eventuality. The signals were for each other, but they took me into their confidence and made sure I could see them.

A ball would go to the keeper rather sluggishly, and the batsman would be given out. Col Egar would casually turn so that I could see him, and nonchalantly rub away at his thumb. The message was clear—the batsman had been caught off his glove, and I could tell the world quickly and surely, without the often inconclusive aid of a TV replay.

Hands together might mean the ball had come off the pad, a touch of the ear might mean it went from bat to pad. Whatever the circumstance, Col or Lou would let me know pretty quickly, and the commentary was much better for it.

Throughout my time in radio I have also made a study of the idiosyncrasies of umpires. More often than not they telegraph their decisions before they actually make them. If I could read their intent, and get in with the decision before they did, I could call a man out before the crowd realised, so the swell of their roar built up behind me. That added so much drama to the broadcast. Egar, for instance, always drew his feet together, as if standing to attention, before he raised his finger to signal a batsman's demise. As soon as those legs came together, I knew. 'He's gone,' I would say, beating the finger and beating the crowd.

It was an almost foolproof system, and one which I never let on about, lest Egar unconsciously changed his *modus operandi*. Other umpires had a habit of crouching before they gave a decision in the affirmative. Others let their hands drop to their sides first. Reading them, I reasoned, was one of the biggest aids to my broadcasting technique.

Rowan and Egar were most conscientious about our communication system. They thought it important their actions were quickly understood, for a start. And they said it relaxed them. Physically nominating the basis for each decision somehow crystallised it in their minds, and made them feel better. I made a point throughout my career of getting as close as I could to the umpires. With that pair it was very easy. They were great men with a great love of cricket, and our morning chats before play became a ritual.

For much of my career, too, I had considerable help from the players. Keith Miller would touch his forehead as he turned to bowl, thereby alerting me to the fact that he was going to let fly a bouncer. I was ready for it. Often I would get in first. A rub on the right side of his nose would nominate the inswinger, a rub to the left side would nominate the outswinger. I could call with certainty so many of the deliveries he bowled, particularly those that were in any way different. So it was with several players.

A BORN LEADER
by Gordon Bray

Gordon Bray began as a trainee broadcaster with the ABC and grew to become one of its leading television commentators, establishing a world class reputation as a Rugby aficionado. He has since followed the Rugby rights to commercial television, where he continues to excel.

GORDON BRAY

A man's man. When he conversed with fellow broadcasters it was as a leader. One who'd captained NSW in a grand era. Always immaculately groomed, always in a freshly starched collar and crisply knotted sporting tie.

On first impression an arch traditionalist, yet always prepared to bend just a little to those he trusted and respected. Mac was a father figure to we young ABC sports broadcasters—a stern taskmaster who could also be an understanding sounding-board. But if he sensed your initiative or enthusiasm weren't close to the boil, then you could expect a knowing and unceremonious prod.

His inspirational advice still rings in my ears with the clarity of a church bell. 'Let your broadcast *breathe*. Work your microphone, and use the crowd!'

I must have heard that McGilvray mantra scores of times, and in a variety of settings. Declaimed at the bar of his favourite watering hole, the Lord Dudley Hotel in Paddington. Intoned in his hotel room on countless tours. Recited with quite dignity in our old offices at 164 William Street, the former headquarters of ABC Sport, a location where the legends of broadcasting loomed at every turn.

To step into Mac's old office, a dingy cubicle which he shared with colourful race caller Geoff Mahoney, was to cross the threshold into a goldmine of sporting knowledge and experience. If you were in luck, you might be invited to sit down, and then there was every chance you'd be whisked away on an hour-long magic carpet ride of reminiscence. Most of us were fond of a modest punt, so first we'd

ABC race caller Geoff Mahoney shared an office with Mac for ten years. Mac was never a punter but he had a high regard for Geoff both as a man and as a broadcaster.

be regaled with the latest antics of 'Curly the Caterpillar' and 'Tommy Tomato', a couple of Geoff's more colourful mates at the track. But pretty soon Mac would pick up the yarn-spinning thread to hypnotise us with tales of 'The Don' or Keith Miller. There was always a story, always a laugh, always a priceless free sporting education to be had in the company of 'Mac and Mahoney'.

As both a teacher and mentor, AD McGilvray was as good as they come. 'You must always beat the crowd,' he would tell us. 'If someone is out, you lift with the snick. Call the catch *before* it hits the fieldsman's hands. If he drops or fumbles you're right there ... "He's caught!" ... "Dropped!" ... or, "Chappell takes it!" *Then* let the crowd sweep the moment away.'

To aim for anticipation in commentary can be a hazardous target to set yourself. Guess wrong and there's nowhere else to go. But, when it comes off, there are few more effective or satisfying moments for a broadcaster. McGilvray elevated the skills of anticipation to the level of an artform. He created word-pictures for his listeners, subtly built expectation in their minds and more often than not delivered the promised outcome. He took the audience out there onto the field with him, visualising proceedings through the eyes of a shrewd and tough former NSW skipper prowling in the slips, missing nothing.

Mac's other decree was to always work closely with the 'expert' commentator. 'Complement each other; feed him appropriate lines,' he'd suggest. 'By the two of you working together the broadcast gains strength.' This McGilvray philosophy of partnership was taken to extraordinary lengths by the master commentator himself. When interstate on Test duty, I often found myself called up to Mac's room at about 8.30 am. There would be a meeting already in progress, the ABC commentary team previewing the coming day's play. Former Test great Norman O'Neill was always in attendance, as was Norman May. Executive producer Alan Marks was also an occasional visitor. This very necessary morning ritual was known as McGilvray's 'prayer meeting'. Several small glasses of beer were consumed, and carefully charged to the ABC (I hope no former Heads of Sport are reading this).

These daily 'think-tank' sessions led to some classic and colourful broadcasting. After the first few overs from the quicks, Mac would venture: 'Norman [O'Neill], I'd be fascinated to hear your thoughts on the likely first change bowler for Australia this morning. I think Peter Taylor might cause real problems on this pitch.' O'Neill's reply: 'I'm glad you've sprung that question on me Alan because I agree with you. In fact I'll be very disappointed if Taylor is not first change.'

What to the listeners must have sounded like casual cricketing banter was, in truth, a considered scenario which had been discussed several times at the 'prayer meeting' two hours earlier. Our audience could only marvel at the 'rapport' between these two great personalities. The daily prayer meetings were a permanent fixture over decades of cricket. Each morning Mac would bring fresh ideas and insights to the debate. His incredible resilience was matched by an enormously fertile sporting mind. Often it was like listening to a university lecture. Those quiet gatherings (and the palate-cleansing ales which accompanied them) were certainly an essential part of my broadcasting education.

But while he was always 'the professor' and our undisputed

Alan Marks had a brief stint with Mac as a Test cricket commentator. He went on to become an award-winning executive producer for ABC Radio Sport.

doyen, Mac still enjoyed the company of the younger broadcasters. His endless stream of anecdotes could be spellbinding—virtually hypnotic—and it was an inability to tear myself away from a McGilvray cricket story which almost proved my undoing. He was holding court one lunchtime at the Gladstone Hotel in William Street (in the old days, the 'Glad' was the ABC's other office—the daily haunt of many of Australia's most celebrated radio actors and broadcasters). I'd been sent down to David Jones by the Director of Sport, the late Bernard Kerr, to pick up his regular loaf of gluten-free bread. On the way back I dropped into the pub to have a quick beer with Mac. Four hours later I was still there but, to my horror, I discovered that some light-fingered health nut had knocked off the gluten-free bread!

Mac consoled me and suggested that rather than confront the boss immediately, it might be a better idea to join him at the Lord Dudley and discuss the matter further. I declined, because through my alcoholic haze I'd somehow managed to calculate that there was still enough time to nip back to DJs and pick up another loaf. But, when I eventually rushed into the Sports Department at 5.45 pm with the replacement loaf, I was informed that Mr Kerr had already left in a huff. Clearly, speedy and decisive action was required.

Forty-five minutes later I disembarked from the Maroubra Express bus. Darkness had descended. When I finally arrived at Mr Kerr's residence, there was no greeting light on the porch. I approached the front door. Suddenly the outside light flashed on with the shocking impact of a police search beam. While my sheepish and still befuddled mind was trying to adapt to the brightness, the front door flew open. Simultaneously, an arm reached out and brusquely snatched the bread from my grasp. In the next instant the door slammed shut and the light flicked off! I stood empty-handed, frozen in time, wondering whether this bizarre episode was to be the final chapter in my brief career as an ABC commentator. Dereliction of duty is a serious charge when you're serving a cadetship. Never again was I asked to pick up Mr Kerr's gluten-free bread, and never again did I risk an extended 'liquid lunch' with the great McGilvray at the Gladstone Hotel.

Alan enjoyed entertaining in his stylish Double Bay apartment after a day's play at the Sydney Cricket Ground. To be asked to attend during a Test match was a special privilege and I'll never forget my first invitation to Mr Mac's kitchen. At stumps on the second day of the Ashes Test of 1971 at the SCG, a flurry of close-of-play drinks already preceded our arrival. Geoff Boycott and John Snow had made life difficult on the field for our boys but there would be no shortage of expertise and advice on hand at the McGilvray household to shape an Australian revival. By the time I'd put names to all the familiar faces in Mac's apartment, I realised a proverbial Who's Who of the cricketing world were present. Commentators from both sides, including the BBC's legendary Brian Johnston (resplendent in a cream suit with complementing two-tone shoes). 'Johnners' was as effusive as ever. Norman May found a comfortable armchair in his favourite corner. The late Jim Burke was there. So too another Australian legend Lindsay Hassett, together with umpire Col Egar and a handful of the 'working' scribes.

Mac's wife Gwen was a wonderful host and I particularly remember her concern for my deteriorating condition as that memorable evening unfolded. As midnight approached, a select group of 'stayers' adjourned to Mac's infamous kitchen. This was where the serious part of the evening always began. My world was already well and truly in a spin, but with an unwavering hand our distinguished host now produced a large bottle of the finest aged Scotch whisky. Once the top was removed (with appropriate ceremony) it was immediately despatched out the window with a flourish, marking a symbolic gesture of challenge. Clearly there was some ritual to be observed. A large glass of the expensive imported fluid was formally handed to me on this, the occasion of my first visit. As the saying goes, the rest is history—or more accurately—I was!

After taking just one gulp I was overwhelmed by an unstoppable urge to seek the restorative qualities of fresh air. I hurtled towards the back door like some demented guided missile and landed outside in the driveway. My last impression was of becoming entangled in one of Mrs Mac's prized rose bushes. Many hours later the chill of Sydney early morning awoke me from deep slumber. I was, as far as I could tell, supine. Face up, but with a nasty dewy sensation along my back. As I lifted my head it banged hard against a sharp steel edge. What on earth was going on? As I winced and turned sideways it was apparent dawn was gently breaking over the Eastern Suburbs. The relaxed chatter of familiar voices was close by. But where precisely *was* I, and who'd just smacked me on the noggin with an iron bar?

The puzzle took another few minutes to solve. I'd collapsed on the median strip of Mac's driveway. At some point later during the night, Keith Miller had arrived and, oblivious of my unorthodox choice of a sleeping place, had parked his car directly on top of me. Miraculously, despite sporting a tyre mark in my trouser leg, there were no apparent breakages or collateral damage (save for my wickedly aching head).

At the end of the Test, which England won by 299 runs, I had sobered up sufficiently to seek advice from Mac about submitting a petty cash claim for my ruined trousers. As always, his reaction in matters of such delicacy was instructive: 'I'd let that one go straight through to the keeper, Master Bray'. There were many other memorable occasions at Mac's kitchen, mainly with ABC colleagues, but none quite matched the impact of that inaugural visit.

Mac became one of the great institutions of Australian cricket. This status was reinforced during the damaging split in the 1970s between the 'traditional' game and the breakaway Kerry Packer 'circus'. The ABC remained loyal to traditional cricket and kept up its comprehensive radio and television broadcasts of the official matches, with McGilvray very much to the fore. During that period the ABC released a memorable record, *The Game is Not the Same*

Without McGilvray. For public consumption, Alan maintained the position that he would never forgive the ABC for releasing the jingle. But for those in the know, the truth was he was really pretty chuffed about it, not that we ever extracted any such admission from the reluctant 'star'.

It wasn't for lack of trying. Often, as the scheduled evening departure from the Lord Dudley Hotel loomed, a few well-meaning stirrers would raise the thorny issue of that ditty just to ruffle his feathers. 'I'm very annoyed with the ABC about the song,' he'd protest. 'I would never have agreed to it and, quite frankly, I can't stand it!' Later, now safely ensconced in *the* kitchen, a scurrilous group of young commentators (containing the likes of Jim Maxwell, Peter Shipway, Peter Longman and yours truly), would urge Mac to bring out his tape of the song and play it for us.

He'd boil. 'How *dare* the ABC involve me in that record. It's so *tasteless!*' But five minutes later we'd all be singing along (the great man included) followed by a series of encores. *That* game will never be the same.

My lasting memories of Alan McGilvray are his sheer strength of character and his remarkably intuitive skills behind the microphone. On the former, he never suffered people he didn't respect. He would not hide behind his feelings under any circumstances. You always got it straight from Mac—firmly and politely. As for those peerless 'on-air' skills, we can now only marvel at the magic of that bygone era when listening to McGilvray describe cricket on the wireless was a national sporting institution. His timing was always absolutely precise and he commanded a special gift of knowing how to capture the moment for maximum impact.

When Mac was trapped in the commentary box at Kingston, Jamaica, during the riots on the 1978 Australian tour, his description of the terrifying sequence of events was riveting. Not only did he paint a graphic word picture, but he did so in a typically composed and courageous manner, fully aware that his words were in all probability being heard outside on the transistor radios of the rioters. Without exaggeration, it was potentially a life and death situation. Thankfully, the calm, reassuring voice of McGilvray was at the controls during one of the most distressing moments in our sporting history.

Whenever I prepare for a Rugby Test commentary on television, I still always pause during the buildup to recall the advice of master broadcaster AD McGilvray.

*Many young broadcasters at the ABC had the benefit of much
McGilvray advice down the years. Gordon Bray makes reference to the
McGilvray determination to be precise, and to integrate with commen-
tary teams to make the broadcast almost personal for the listener.*

*This art was the fulcrum of ABC cricket through several generations,
in which Alan McGilvray gradually became the centre of the whole
operation.*

The following extract from The Game Goes On *gives an insight into
the lessons McGilvray learned, the manner in which he formed his
commentary partnerships, and the way in which times have changed.*

ALAN McGILVRAY

One early lesson I had was from the great Australian left-hander
of the early 1900s, Warren Bardsley, who button-holed me at
the SCG one day and poured forth his displeasure. With a cricket
bat, Warren was a joy to behold. Off the field, he was a little
more rough around the edges, a fellow who said what he thought.
'You talk too much,' he told me. 'Just tell us where the ball
went, who fielded it, how many they scored. That's all. Just give
us the score and tell us what happened. That's all we want.' It
was a good lesson, if not totally appreciated at the time.

In those early days the broadcasting of cricket in Australia
was a truly measured art. I recall the early lessons I received
from Charles Moses, whom I regard as the first really great influence on sports broadcasting in Australia. He wanted expertise
and a certain intimacy. A communion with the listener that not
only informed him, but almost took him into a confidence.
'Involve the people,' he would say, 'and make them feel part of
it.'

This approach required a certain stability from the commentary team. Above all it required teamwork. We developed that
in the early days when Vic Richardson and Arthur Gilligan were
involved. We kept it going through the expertise of men like
Johnny Moyes and Lindsay Hassett. I was privileged to work
with these people and to develop with them a rapport by which
we fed off each other. We knew how to draw each other out—
how to get to the meat of a subject in such a way that the listener

could feel actually involved in the discussion. This was our aim, at least, and the most necessary component of it was the fact that we were a team, operating together, pretty well all the time.

I always felt that sort of broadcasting served Australia well. I am sure it built traditions by which both the Australian Broadcasting Commission and the game of cricket became an integral part of the Australian way of life. It was always going to be that way, I suppose, for the people who shaped ABC cricket commentary through those early days insisted on standards that were very high indeed. I was very lucky to have happened along when I did, when there was still a pioneering element to what we were doing, and grateful that I had the chance to work, through the ABC, with a game I loved. It was the case with all of us through most of my fifty-odd years of ABC involvement. Men like Sir Charles Moses and Sir Talbot Duckmanton, who ran the ABC as successive general managers, were very particular that those involved knew their subject. ABC commentary was entrusted only to those who were undeniably expert in their field. And it became a fairly select bunch, developing a personality of its own, and a form of teamwork which eventually left the listeners with the feeling that they knew us all well.

The ABC in recent times has let that philosophy slip. Times change and pressures re-arrange themselves and intrusions such as television have, of course, made a difference to the modern perceptions of radio cricket. But I still find it regrettable that the ABC has let those old standards go. In my last years there I found it difficult to work, for instance, with such a variety of co-commentators that I could never get a feel for their thinking. One season towards the end I think I worked with eight different summarisers. In the days of Lindsay Hassett there was an affinity which allowed us to get to the heart of any subject very quickly indeed. We knew each other and we knew each other's minds. In later years I found it harder to inform our listeners by means of conversation with a summariser, because there were so many of them, and it was never possible to get that intuitive feel of how they might answer, how we might best get to the points that needed to be made.

There is a modern theory that specialisation is not a good thing. Everybody should have a bit of a go here and a bit of a go there, and this is the sort of thinking that has invaded the ABC in its presentation of sport. Most of the commentators involved are highly professional and very good and I certainly have the highest respect for men like Norman O'Neill, with whom I worked a lot in my latter years with the ABC. He knows the game as well as anyone. But the point remains that the ABC, in the broad sense, was nowhere near as particular in the late 'eighties about building and maintaining a stable, authoritative commentary team as it once was. Names bob up and disappear, people come and go, and the credibility of the exercise suffers. More's the pity, for I doubt there are many Australians who lived through the first seventy-five years or so of the twentieth century who would not agree that the broadcasting of cricket through the Australian Broadcasting Commission was a very identifiable part of the Australian way of life.

A SUMMER TRUST
by Mark Ray

Mark Ray is a long-term cricket devotee who made it to the first-class arena and became a noted cricket journalist with the Sunday Age. *His most recent book,* Border and Beyond, *was published by ABC Books in 1995.*

MARK RAY

Each summer, like most Australian kids, I played backyard cricket every weekday after school. When you could only play official competition cricket for three hours each Saturday morning, those backyard games were essential for our mental health. They eased our hunger for the real stuff and allowed us to fantasise about leading the wonderful life of a Test cricketer. Although there were only two of us—Steve, the kid from up the street, and I—we had plenty of company. Our games were peopled by a cast of dozens of the world's greatest players. What I realised only after Alan McGilvray's recent death was that he was also there, his mellow, wise commentary adding the ultimate note of reality to our Test matches.

Whoever won the toss would be Australia—Lawry, Simpson, Harvey, O'Neill, Booth, Burge, Cowper (I was a left-hander so Cowper, Lawry and Harvey made most of the runs), McKenzie, Davidson (most of the wickets) and the great skipper, Richie Benaud. Whoever lost the toss was compensated by being allowed to pretend for a couple of hours that he was Frank Worrell, Gary Sobers, Wes Hall, Lance Gibbs or Fred Trueman, Brian Statham, Ken Barrington and even that quintessential posh Pom, Ted Dexter.

As Steve, in the persona of Wes Hall, would walk back to his mark up against the side fence and dip the tennis ball into the bucket of water (our way of simulating the new ball), I would assume McGilvray's role as radio commentator while also ducking and weaving in Bill Lawry mode. The commentary would begin quietly, coolly, almost in a whisper and build to a climax as Big Wes thumped another one into the concrete slab that was our unforgiving pitch.

'And Lawry's taken that one in the ribs. A nasty delivery that lifted off a length at great speed. As ever Lawry doesn't flinch.'

And so it went for hours, one afternoon's play rolling into the next until each of five Test matches was won, lost or drawn. Most kids, I'm sure, did something similar and most would have added commentary. Without it the games would have lacked the right rhythm, the measured, remorseless flow with occasional bursts of high drama that sets Test cricket apart from other games. This was before television arrived to replay and dissect every delivery and before one-day cricket changed the rhythm. Every year my parents and I went to the first day of the Sydney Test, and perhaps to a day or two of a Sheffield Shield match. That was all the big cricket we saw. For the rest we had to rely on an accurate radio call and there was only one voice that would do. And of course, every four years there was the added delight of an Ashes tour when at night McGilvray's familiar voice would come crackling across the sea from England.

McGilvray's work came to occupy such a central and intimate place in my cricket world that I remember only two of his co-commentators, the superb Lindsay Hassett and the great Englishman, John Arlott. The rest did not register. McGilvray's was the voice of Australian cricket. He seemed to control its rhythm. He was the trusted guide who told us what was really happening way out there on the field. Without McGilvray our boyhood games would have been mere backyard frolics, not Test matches.

As boyhood turned into adolescence Saturday morning games came to be followed by afternoon matches in the men's competition and weekday afternoons were spent in the school nets. Our backyard Test series faded. But Alan McGilvray's voice was still with us as we sat in the shade of a tree or in a car watching our teammates bat on the matting pitches in the local suburban afternoon competition. I suppose it was the only way that we felt related, however distantly, to the greats who played for Australia. McGilvray's commentary reminded us that we were all playing the same game, no matter how wide the gap in standards that separated Test players from those sweating it out on parks all over Australia every Saturday arvo.

Most of all, from the late 1960s to his retirement in the mid-1980s, the first time every summer we heard Alan McGilvray's voice meant only one thing: summer had arrived and so the cricket was back again. The English poet John Keats wrote in his 'Ode To A Nightingale' of 'the murmurous haunt of flies on summer eves'. Is it stretching things too far to say that the arrival of McGilvray's mellow tones each summer sounded just as musical? To my parents and me, and other cricket lovers all over Australia, it was surely one of the most reassuring of sounds. We might have enjoyed the football and the winter's break, but cricket was our game, summer our season.

For a decade or so after those Saturday afternoons, Alan McGilvray's voice travelled with me every summer even though at times I barely noticed. It was just always there—in the background while studying at home, competing against the sound of waves at a beach, there on a transistor behind the school nets when we were having a hit or again on a transistor as a mate and I hitchhiked on one of those long, dusty, flat roads in the central west of New South Wales.

Then in the early 1980s I became more aware of McGilvray's constant presence when I realised he might actually have mentioned my own name on air. I'd played a few first-class games at the Sydney Cricket Ground and when a friend said that he had heard McGilvray mention me, I was struck by the honour. It was a link, however remote, to the history of the game, almost as valuable as being allowed to use the dressing room that once had been home to people like Victor Trumper, Don Bradman, Bill O'Reilly and, of course, McGilvray himself. I should have asked someone to tape some of the commentary just to hear that voice note my presence, but you never think of those things until it's too late.

After I began working as a cricket journalist, McGilvray was present only in reputation and anecdote. I never saw him in the press box, but often you would hear one of the older cricket writers or some of his successors on ABC Radio tell a story about 'Mac', as he was known to everyone in that world. The reputation was that of a meticulously prepared commentator, always well informed and deserving of the respect he obviously enjoyed. They said he had been hard but fair—surely the best compliment a journalist can earn—and a man who carried himself with dignity, as you would expect after hearing that voice. Those who had toured with him also told the famous stories of how, if he liked and respected you, he would invite you to his hotel room for a drink. That drink was whisky and you would insult the venerable gentleman if you tried to leave before the last drop was gone. These were serious invitations and the memory of them always set heads shaking.

Perhaps the most striking aspect of those invitations was that they often extended to players. And the players knew they also had to abide by the rules. In those days there was far less cricket than there is today. The cricket world was a less hurried place. Journalists and

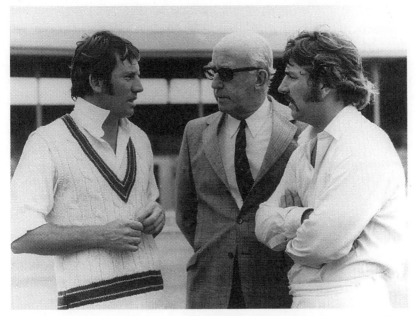

Left to right: Ian Chappell, Mac and Rod Marsh. Players and journalists mixed and socialised more freely in Mac's time, and with the possible exception of Doug Walters, no players were closer to Mac than these two. On this occasion the discussion is serious and almost certainly tactical.

players socialise occasionally these days, but nowhere near as freely nor as often as they did in McGilvray's time. The pressures are too great now, the stakes too high. The money is big, the analysis of a day's play exhaustive, the attitudes of a player's personal sponsors critical. A little bad press can cause a lot of trouble. Or so it seems anyway. As the years pass these pressures will increase and the idea of a commentator chatting as a mate with the players in the dressing room after a day's play or for hours back at the hotel will seem foreign indeed.

Perhaps that is a good thing anyway. With big money comes controversy, rampant egos and the possibility of corruption. Certainly a press journalist is better to keep a little distance from those about whom he is writing. It is probably different for radio or television commentators whose work centres almost exclusively on the action on the field, although that does not make them immune from falling out of favour with players. In recent years Australia's players seem to have been more upset with comments from the Channel 9 commentators—all ex-Test players—than with articles in the press.

Still, it is fair to say that Alan McGilvray was from a different time and so occupied a different place in the structure of the game. Not that he avoided expressing strong opinions. There were plenty of those in his hugely successful books and I was happy on a couple of occasions to quote those judgements in some of my own work. After all, if you could not trust Alan McGilvray whom could you trust?

One of the great strengths of Alan McGilvray's longevity as a commentator was his ability to adapt to changing times. Mark Ray makes reference to the 'changing rhythms' involved in one-day cricket, and alludes to the fact that McGilvray was in his element in the more analytical commentary involved in Test matches. McGilvray, indeed, was originally uncomfortable with one-day cricket and its more contrived pace, but saw its value as time passed. In his book The Game Goes On, *McGilvray enunciated his attitude to the burgeoning power of limited-overs cricket.*

ALAN McGILVRAY

At the end of my days as a broadcaster I suppose it is fair to say I was not a fan of one-day cricket. In many ways it offended my sensibilities, for there was too much slather and whack, too little concern for the traditional trials of strength that were the base of the cricket I had known. Above all, I hated broadcasting it. It had no patterns, and there was no time to paint the word pictures and analyse things as I had always done with traditional cricket. It was a game for calculators and equations. You needed to be a mathematician rather than a tactician, measuring overs bowled and balls remaining and runs required. It just wasn't cricket. Not real cricket, anyway.

Since retirement has given me more time in front of the television set, I have come to modify these early opinions, for there is much about one-day cricket that can be absorbing. And it is getting better. Players are realising it is not necessarily a matter of shutting the eyes and swinging the bat. Bowlers are having more of a say in things. The subtleties of the first class game that seemed to have no place in the new cricket form have crept back, and the games are much more interesting as a result.

The 1987 series of one-day games in which Australia, England, Pakistan and New Zealand competed in Perth as part of the America's Cup celebrations provided a good example. Here there was always a chance for a bowler. The pitch had not been tailored so that players could bat on it for a month, as one-day pitches often are, and the breezes of Perth gave their customary encouragement to bowlers good enough to use them. The consequence was engrossing cricket, in which the bowlers again were probing and testing, and to score quickly against them needed batting of real quality. The Nine network television coverage, with its splendid use of cameras and imagination, made it all very real, and the entertainment value was marvellous.

One-day cricket has been entrenched for quite a few years now as a significant, perhaps even dominant feature of the Australian summer sporting calendar. Those traditionalists who scoffed at it have to realise that it won't go away. And the reason it won't is the most positive reason of all. People like it. Crowds beyond our imagination a few years ago throng to see it. And it brings to the cricketing world an excitement and an entertainment level that clearly fill a modern need.

When it all started in the turmoil of World Series Cricket, I was one of many sceptics. It intruded on my established perceptions of what cricket was all about. It upset the rhythm of my experience, and I suppose in the broad sense it threatened me, for it turned over the values of a lifetime and ate away at the basic tenets on which Test cricket had survived for more than a century. It was producing loose batting. It was killing off technique. And ultimately it would tear the insides out of our Test match capability. It seemed a contrived, plastic sort of thing in which bowlers were reduced to cart horses, denied the normal support fields that helped them chase wickets. They were forced to become dull and negative, and batsmen had to slog willy-nilly to cope.

Much of that remains true in varying degrees today. But there is a process of adaptation going on that is making one-day cricket more acceptable, even to the most hard-nosed traditionalists. As players have worked it all out there is less loose and undisciplined batting than there used to be. The value of wickets has re-emerged to a certain extent. But above all the game has given the public a type of cricket they obviously want. I confess to enjoying it—the better games, anyway. And the manner in which crowds have flocked to it on a continuing basis is evidence enough that cricket has to take stock of itself and prepare for the inevitable evolutionary processes that the twenty-first century will entail.

A PERMANENT PRESENCE

by John Howard

John Howard was elected Prime Minister of Australia in March 1996. He has been a long-time cricket buff, a regular at the Sydney Cricket Ground Test matches over many years. Like so many other Australians, he grew up to the sounds of Alan McGilvray at the cricket.

JOHN HOWARD

Until his retirement from cricket broadcasting only a few years ago, Alan McGilvray had been quite inseparable from my own consciousness of the game of cricket. Quite simply, he had always been there. From the moment I began listening to ABC cricket broadcasts, during the 1946–47 MCC tour of Australia by England then led by Walter Hammond, Alan McGilvray was always part and parcel of ABC cricket coverage.

In those pre-television days he formed a remarkable partnership with Johnnie Moyes and Victor Richardson. Arthur Gilligan was the English contribution to that broadcasting quartet. Charles Fortune and Ernest Eytle substituted for Gilligan when the West Indies or South African tours took place.

There were many things which could be said about Alan McGilvray's broadcasting skills. He had authority, precision and above all, enjoyed great respect. Having been a first-class cricketer himself, he brought natural understanding and credibility to his broadcasts. He was present during the infancy of radio broadcasts of Test cricket between Australia and England.

His coverage was meticulous, but never boring. He did have a special capacity to enliven a dull patch during a match. Equally, however, he had both the seniority and the credibility to speak his mind very bluntly if he thought that tactics being used or behaviour being indulged in were unworthy of the game. I particularly recall some scathing remarks during his commentary on the 1958–59 tour

Johnny Moyes (left), and Ernest Eytle covering the West Indies tour of Australia in 1951–52. Eytle was the first West Indian to be a guest commentator for ABC Radio in Australia.

of Australia by England. That time Peter May led the MCC. McGilvray was particularly critical of the stonewall tactics of the English opener, Trevor Bailey. The first Test of that series had been notoriously dull and instead of trying to explain it all away with soothing phrases, Alan McGilvray was sharply critical of the English tactics used, particularly those of Bailey. From recollection, Australia was set a reasonably modest target to win during the fourth innings. It was one of Norman O'Neill's earlier Test matches. He performed particularly well and helped knock off most of the runs required, with McGilvray loud and frequent in his praise of O'Neill's positive approach.

Alan McGilvray was, of course, a passionate advocate of Australian cricket, and always enthused when Australia was successful. However, this did not lead him to be a blindly partisan commentator or one who saw no skill or merit in players or teams or other countries. In fact, McGilvray was immaculately fair and objective in all of his commentaries. No doubt his long years describing the game which covered many ups and downs of Australian cricket, induced a sense of balance and long-sightedness absent from commentators whose time at the microphone has been more compressed.

I always associate Alan McGilvray with hot summers. If you loved sport in the 1950s listening to cricket and/or the Davis Cup,

from Boxing Day onwards was the beginning and end of your exis-
tence. As I reflect upon the numerous cricketing broadcasts I have
heard, Alan McGilvray was there at just about all of them. Ironically
though, his then Brisbane ABC colleague, Clive Harburg, was at the
microphone during the final over of the historic tied Test in Brisbane
in 1960 between Australia and the West Indies.

McGilvray helped describe both the triumphs and defeats expe-
rienced by Australian cricketers over a period of 50 years. He followed
the unbeaten 1948 team. I can vividly recall his description of our
despair during the Old Trafford Test of 1956 when Jim Laker captured
19 of the 20 Australian wickets that fell.

Like so many people who follow cricket, he was caught up in
the turbulent events of the late 1970s which saw the birth of World
Series Cricket, a temporary schism in the game and the re-emergence
of cricket in a stronger, more diverse form which has gathered new
followers whilst preserving traditional patterns of the game. In the
early years of television coverage of Test cricket, it was not infre-
quently that people would remark that they watched the television
coverage with the sound turned down and the ABC radio commentary

Clive Harburg, the ABC Queensland Sporting Supervisor, was the commentator for
the last over of the fabulous Tied Test in Brisbane, 1960. Here he demonstrates to
his son a straight, but ancient, bat.

on so that Alan McGilvray's commentary was still available.

I met Alan McGilvray for the first time towards the end of his long broadcasting career. In recent years, I saw him frequently at the Sydney Cricket Ground. The last of those occasions was during the third Test in January 1995 between England and Australia which ended at 7.25 pm on the last day as an absorbing draw. Incidentally, that game attracted almost 30 000 spectators on that day, rather giving the lie to those who assert that traditional Test matches are on the way out! During my conversations at that Test with Alan McGilvray he spoke enthusiastically about Shane Warne's tremendous skills, but characteristically he had high praise for the entertaining Englishman Darren Gough.

It is something of a cliché to describe a person as an ornament to the game of cricket. To use that description of Alan McGilvray is, I know, to express the views of millions of Australian cricket followers as a consequence of his broadcasts.

The famous Tied Test of 1960 was both a high point and a low point of Alan McGilvray's broadcasting career. As John Howard points out, McGilvray missed the climax of that remarkable game between the West Indies under Frank Worrell, and Australia under Richie Benaud, and thus the opportunity to describe one of the great pieces of cricket history.

This is the account of that day which he gave in The Game Is Not The Same . . .

ALAN McGILVRAY

It had looked all over for the Australians when Hall had ripped through their second innings to leave them 6–92. Australia was chasing 233 and things looked grim. Then Benaud joined Alan Davidson, and the value of a couple of good all-rounders was never better in evidence than in their partnership of 134. That took the score to 226—seven runs needed to win. A brilliant piece of work by Joe Solomon ran out Davidson. New man Wally Grout took a single off the first ball then faced Wes Hall for that last over. As might be said these days in the vernacular of modern television and the one-day scrambles, the equation then read: Runs needed 6, balls remaining 8, wickets in hand 3.

History has well recorded that last over. I have listened to the tape of Clive Harburg's description over and over again. It is magic cricket.

First Ball: Grout hit on leg. No time to worry about that however, since Benaud calls him for a single with the ball stationary about a yard from the stumps. They make it. The equation now reads five runs wanted, seven balls remaining, three wickets standing.

Second Ball: Hall lets fly a bouncer. Benaud swings to hook. A faint touch of the glove and 'keeper Gerry Alexander roars his appeal for the catch. Benaud out for 52. Still five runs wanted, six balls to come, two wickets in hand.

Third Ball: Ian Meckiff plays it without a run. Still five runs wanted, five balls left.

Fourth Ball: Meckiff fails to make contact and Grout, taking off like Jesse Owens, calls for a bye. Four balls left, four runs to get, still two wickets standing.

Fifth Ball: Grout goes on to the back foot looking for his favourite hook shot. The ball is too far up for it but still he swings and the ball flies high into the air at square leg. Kanhai moves to get under it but ducks out of the way as the big frame of Wesley Hall comes at him trying to make the catch. Hall drops it. The batsmen scurry through for a single. Three runs wanted, three balls to go.

Sixth Ball: Hall, somewhat heart-broken, moves in again. By now a certain amount of pandemonium has broken out in the crowd. This time Meckiff swings across the flight of the ball, somehow manages to connect and the ball flies high towards the mid-wicket boundary. Clive Harburg calls the four. The match looks over. But the grass in the outfield had not been cut that morning and a patch of clover slows up the ball sufficiently to allow Conrad Hunte to field. The batsmen have completed two and turned for three as Hunte picks up. It looks safe enough. Meckiff has the speed but Grout hasn't. The ball flies to Alexander's gloves and the bails are off before Grout, diving full length, is anywhere near his crease. The batsmen had crossed for their third run, so two counted and the scores were level. Two balls remain. One wicket standing.

By this time confusion reigned. The scoreboard attendants had no idea what was happening. The players weren't sure how many runs were needed. But the umpires Col Hoy and Colin Egar, whose poise and concentration were unbelievable through those final overs, had command of the situation throughout.

Lindsay Kline joined Ian Meckiff for the seventh delivery.

Kline played it towards mid-wicket. Meckiff called him. Solomon gathered fifteen yards out. There was nobody at the wicket to take his throw. Alexander, standing back to Hall's pace, had no hope of getting there. Frank Worrell saw that and raced to the bowler's end and called for the ball. It was a certain run-out at that end since Kline had been late in responding to Meckiff's call. But the noise at the time was deafening. The crowd was screaming. The players were screaming. Solomon had no hope of hearing his skipper's call. He threw to the wicket-keeper's end. He had the width of no more than one and a half stumps to hit from his side-on position.

In perhaps the most significant piece of fielding in the history of Test cricket, little Joe Solomon's throw homed in on the stumps like a laser beam. Meckiff was still a yard short and umpire Hoy's finger went up. Australia all out 232. Scores level. Match tied. The first tie in Test cricket.

In the pandemonium that followed few people realised it was a tie. The West Indies players dashed off the field thinking they had won. Worrell was shouting at them 'No, we haven't won'. Nobody could hear him. The Australians thought they had lost. Meckiff was furious with himself for getting run out. Benaud ran on the ground to shake Frank Worrell's hand. The skippers knew the result, and as it sank in all over the country, the success of Frank Worrell's tour was assured.

Now I can assure you my account of the last moments of that Test is a faithful one. As I said, I have listened to the broadcast a hundred times. I have discussed that final over with every man who took part. I have listened entranced to their various accounts of it. Through the rest of that tour we talked about it again and again. If I didn't raise the question of it to satisfy my thirst for information as to what actually went through the players' minds, they made sure they related the drama of it to me. And they did so with a touch of sadistic pleasure.

For the fact is I missed it. I wasn't there. In what must rank as the greatest error of judgment in my life, I left the ground with a couple of hours to go on that fateful afternoon to catch an early plane back to Sydney. My broadcasting commitments had finished for the day, and with Australia heading to a seemingly certain defeat in the early afternoon, Keith Miller and I decided we would head back to Sydney on the last flight, rather than wait in Brisbane the extra day. As we neared Sydney the hostess in the aircraft volunteered to us the news that the match had finished 'even'.

'You mean it was a draw?' Miller asked. 'No, it wasn't a draw' she replied. 'Then the West Indies won?' Miller offered. 'No, nobody won it' she said. 'I'll go back and find out.'

By the time she returned with confirmation Miller and I had canvassed the possibility of the only other result—a tie—and were in the process of attacking a bottle of scotch and convincing ourselves it simply could not be.

It was, of course, and I don't think I have ever really got over it. I have spent nearly twenty-five years being furious with myself for leaving Brisbane that day. Never again have I left a Test match early.

THE GAME IS NOT THE SAME

by Norman Tasker

*Norman Tasker is a cricket writer of long experience,
having been a confrere of McGilvray on tours at home
and abroad from 1968 until 1980. He collaborated with
McGilvray on four books*—The Game Is Not The Same,
The Game Goes On, Back Page of Cricket *and* Captains
Of The Game. *These days, among other things, he is
managing editor of* Inside Edge *magazine, and sports
editor of* The Bulletin.

NORMAN TASKER

BY the time the caravan reached Hove for the game against Sussex
on the 1972 Australian team's tour of England, spirits were fairly high.
Ian Chappell's team had lost the first Test at Old Trafford, won the
second handsomely at Lord's and had much the better of a drawn
third Test at Trent Bridge. In the process the Englishmen under Ray
Illingworth had shown more than a little frailty against the emerging
pace of Dennis Lillee and the superb swing bowling of Bob Massie,
who had devastated them in a 16-wicket haul at Lord's. England knew
that if they were to prevail and continue the dominace they had shown
against Australia in 1970–71, drastic measures were called for.

　　Hove is one of those places on a tour of England which offers a
little rest and recreation through the grind of an exacting Test series.
The cricket on offer from a county like Sussex is competitive enough,
but the atmosphere of necessity is relaxed. The deckchairs and the
marquees make for a pleasant day out, and to travelling journalists
and commentators confronted with the rather less stressful requirements of a minor match, the convivial conversation of the bar becomes
an ever present temptation. I was travelling with the team as cricket
writer for the *Sun* newspaper in Sydney, and evening deadlines made
this a day for scouting about, talking to people, soaking up the ambi-
ence. From a journalist's view-point, there was more to be achieved

Mac and Norm Tasker—tour buddies and literary collaborators.

by communicating with those at the coalface than there was by spending the day half asleep in the press box. When Alan McGilvray appeared, similarly relaxed and anxious for a beer and a chat, you knew the day would provide a fund of insights, of information, of anecdotes and of plain good comradeship. Play was just under way, the sun was high in the sky, our priorities had been safely analysed . . . what else to do but adjourn to the bar?

Alan loved such days. Cricket was not something he turned on and off when a microphone was in front of him. It was a consuming passion that blended his work and his life into one package. Talking cricket with his friends was a part of him, and he was never short of an audience among the many fellow travellers who admired his knowledge and marvelled at the clarity of his understanding. On this particular day the conversation had been especially bouyant, as was befitting Australians in tow with a young team on the brink of re-establishing lost dominance over the Old Enemy. A new wave was building here, with names like Lillee, Greg Chappell, Rodney Marsh and Co in full cry.

During the course of the day England's team was announced for the fourth Test at Headingley. It included the name of Derek Underwood, the left-arm spin bowler who had been highly successful against the previous Australian team to tour, and who was noted as a bowler to exploit anything untoward in a pitch. As McGilvray looked at the name, you could almost hear the alarm bells going off in his head. Underwood had been discarded from the team, and had done nothing at all to warrant a recall. Mac came up with a likely scenario in an instant. The pitch would be a bad one. An Underwood pitch. The only question to be answered was whether a bad pitch was an accident, and Underwood's selection had merely followed to take advantage. Or whether some human intervention had taken place; whether some dastardly scheme had been hatched to make a pitch that would dull the effectiveness of Lillee and Massie and, by implication, provide a bowler of Underwood's type with ideal conditions in which to work.

The Sydney *Sun* cricket writer had his story for the day. Why was Underwood chosen? Does it beg the question as to whether a pitch had been constructed for him? Doctored even? Was this a dastardly scheme to rip the wheels from the Australian bandwagon, just

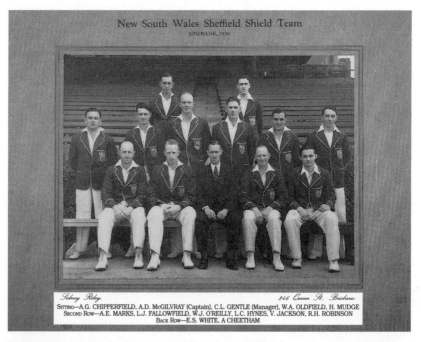

New South Wales Sheffield Shield Team
BRISBANE, 1936

Sidney Riley.   246 Queen St. Brisbane.

SITTING—A.G. CHIPPERFIELD, A.D. McGILVRAY (Captain), C.L. GENTLE (Manager), W.A. OLDFIELD, H. MUDGE
SECOND ROW—A.E. MARKS, L.J. FALLOWFIELD, W.J. O'REILLY, L.C. HYNES, V. JACKSON, R.H. ROBINSON
BACK ROW—E.S. WHITE, A CHEETHAM

Mac was humble about his own cricketing prowess but he was a solid first-class performer who captained NSW for several seasons during one of the greatest eras in Australian cricket.

as it was reaching top speed? The editor back home, of course, made the most of it, and it became the most prophetic story of the tour. In the event of course, the pitch was the famous 'fuserium pitch', Underwood was unplayable, and Australia was ravaged. McGilvray's insight had picked the scenario as soon as he saw the team, such was his intuitive wisdom in these matters; such was his experience and his understanding of cricket minds.

He recounted the events thus in *The Game Is Not The Same*:

ALAN McGILVRAY

The fourth Test at Headingley produced another of those distasteful pitch controversies which seem to thwart Australia so often in England. I recall some mild surprise in the Australian team when we were at Hove shortly before the fourth Test and the England selectors hoisted Derek Underwood into their team. Underwood was a highly dangerous left-arm spin bowler on English wickets. He had taken 7–50 in the final Test against Australia at the Oval in 1968, thanks to the assistance of 1500 'groundsmen' who mopped up the field after a fierce rainstorm. That won the Test and levelled the series against Bill Lawry's team.

Greg Chappell regarded Underwood as the best exploiter of a suspect wicket of any bowler in England. But in 1972 there seemed no reason why he should suddenly be brought from nowhere to join the Test side. They had been travelling along reasonably well, basing their attack on the pace of John Snow, the seamers of Geoff Arnold, the medium-pace of Tony Greig and the off-spin of Illingworth. My first reaction when I saw Underwood's name in the England team was to assume they knew something about the Headingley pitch that we didn't.

I shall never forget our first sight of that Leeds strip. A group of Australian players, some pressmen and myself went out together the day before the game to look at it. It was white and devoid of grass, and looked worse for the fact that it was surrounded by lush turf on all sides. I took a cricket ball and bounced it onto the pitch. It registered a dull thump, and would hardly bounce at all, rising to less than knee height. Ian Chappell just shook his head. Six inches off the pitch we could make the ball bounce chest high.

On every tour I have made to England there has been some sort of problem with the Leeds pitch. We accosted the grounds-men about it there and then. All sorts of excuses were put forward. There had been a rainstorm the previous weekend which flooded it and restricted use of the heavy roller; the pitch had been infested by a fungus called fuserium, which had killed off the grass. Amazingly, it did not seem to affect the turf around it.

Whatever the reasons, Underwood's selection proved a mar-vellous coup for England. He had four wickets in the first innings and six in the second, and England were simply much better equipped to take advantage of unusual conditions than were Australia. England won by nine wickets and the Australian dream of taking home the Ashes was lost.

As a man with an ear to the ground, Alan McGilvray had many advan-tages. To a commentator or a journalist—and deep down Alan looked upon himself as a bit of both—information is his lifeblood. It flowed to McGilvray in a constant stream, such was his standing with every-body in the game, and such was the trust which he engendered. Mac seemed to be so much at the centre of the game that he was a part of most things that happened. Administrators discussed things with him before they acted on them; players discussed their problems; umpires discussed their difficulties. Mac seemed to know everything, not just because he had been told, but often because he had been involved, in one way or another, along the way.

Very early in the piece I learned to my cost it was not wise to question McGilvray information. On the 1970–71 England tour of Australia, the opening first-class match was played at the Adelaide Oval, against South Australia. Colin Egar was the top Australian umpire of the time, and stood in this game, with a long summer stretching ahead of him. He had been a familiar figure in Test matches for more than a decade, and had had his share of controversies. It was Egar, after all, who had no-balled Ian Meckiff in the famous Brisbane Test of 1963. But he was the best, and he would be there for whatever

Mac was a left-handed bat and a right-arm medium pace swing bowler.

controversies Ray Illingworth's team might bring to the Test series. Or so we all assumed.

On the night the match ended, Egar and McGilvray gathered in McGilvray's room at the old Adelaide Travelodge for their customary after-match post mortem. They had become firm friends down the years; Alan developed a strong rapport with umpires, not just because it helped him to understand their work on the field, and thus provided some split second advantages in his commentary, but also because he felt for them as somewhat peripheral figures in the hustle and bustle of big cricket. He saw them at the edge, much as he saw himself, and he felt an affinity that so many of them respected and nurtured. Egar certainly did, and the post mortem in which they indulged at the Travelodge that night made the point.

Covering the tour for my newspaper back in Sydney, I was staying at the bigger Travelodge next door. About 3 am the phone rang, and despite my half awake state there was no mistaking the voice. 'Get down here . . . we've something to tell you.'

A McGilvray command was never to be lightly brushed aside, so down I went to find McGilvray and Egar with glasses in their hands and a glow on their faces. Egar was standing as best he could, a slight rhythmic swaying announcing the fact that this particular post match discussion had been very intense indeed.

'You tell him Col,' McGilvray exhorted. 'If you won't let me talk you out of it, you tell him.' Egar then proceeded, in a very roundabout sort of way, to announce his retirement as an umpire. 'Very silly,' McGilvray interjected. 'Still the best in the business. Very silly.'

It was such an incongruous scene that I found it impossible to take seriously. I helped myself to a drink, conversed erratically for 20 minutes or so, then took myself back to the bed from which I had been summarily summoned. 'Retire indeed,' I thought. 'He won't even remember in the morning.' Unprofessionally (or was it because there was a plane to catch?) I failed to check the night's garbled events next day, and flew off blissfully to Melbourne. McGilvray meanwhile was on the phone, summoning a host of luminaries from Don Bradman down to try to change Egar's mind. They couldn't.

It hit the papers in Melbourne a day or so later. It was big news. I vowed never again to question McGilvray information.

* * * * *

As host, Alan McGilvray was a quite legendary character. Like his great mate Keith Miller, he had a capacity to relate with Prime Ministers and princes with the same, easy rapport that he would find with a young cricketer, or just a fan along the way who would button-hole him for an opinion. His circle of friends was an ever-growing 'who's who' of cricket, who together with his broadcasting mates, his journalist mates, and just his mates, were a constant source of enrichment for him.

When he gathered them in numbers—whether in his room on tour, at the barbecues at his Double Bay home which became a part of every summer, or simply at an impromptu late night gathering in his kitchen—the conversation flowed with a warmth and good humour that set cricket on a higher plain. Small armies of forceful characters would grace these occasions. Freddie Trueman debating matters with Keith Miller, or Norman May arguing tactics with Norman O'Neill . . . always the spirit was lively and the camaraderie genuine, and in the middle of it all McGilvray would be the final oracle, massaging the subjects and enliv-ening the debate with a depth of wisdom and experience that nobody else in the room ever seemed to be able to match.

Above all Alan used to love to tell the stories of his youth; of his own cricket at a time when legends seemed to be at every turn, and he played in a NSW Sheffield Shield team (which he later cap-tained) that reeked class. McGilvray never considered himself to be at the same level as those in whose company he found himself—

Kippax, McCabe, Oldfield, O'Reilly, Bradman—but he was there nevertheless, and he eventually led them well. Those who played with the inimitable Bradman all have stories to tell. Some of them tell them grudgingly, for Bradman is often spoken of as a distant character that his peers found difficult to know. McGilvray conceded some of this; but for the most part, when Bradman's name came up, he looked back with pride at the associations he had had with him, on and off the field. One of the often told stories in the McGilvray kitchen was of the first Shield game he played. He recounted it in *The Game Is Not The Same*.

ALAN McGILVRAY

I was privileged to bat with Bradman in my first game for New South Wales in the summer of 1933–34. We were playing Victoria at the Melbourne Cricket Ground and were something like three down for 199 on the third morning when the new ball became due.

'You open for your club, don't you young man?' our skipper Alan Kippax inquired of me before play. I told him I did. 'Well, you can go in with Bradman,' he ordered. 'And I don't want to see you before lunch.'

Bradman had about twenty runs at the time, and with five seasons as an established Australian batsman already under his belt, he was then very much the No 1 commodity of Australian cricket. It is difficult to describe how I felt that morning, making my way to the wicket with Bradman for my first class debut in front of 40 000 spectators. Kippax had asked Bradman to look after me. Victoria had some fairly useful bowlers in Ironmonger, Blackie and Fleetwood-Smith, and it seemed logical that Don should take most of the strike anyway.

Certainly, that was the way the crowd wanted it. My turns at strike were often greeted with roars of 'out of the way, redhead' or words to that effect, so that Bradman's talents could be projected uninterrupted. So much of the Bradman I later came to know so well was evident that day. I remember the Victorian captain Bill Woodfull saying to me as I stood at the non-striker's end: 'Just how do you stop this man?'

Bradman ran to 100 before lunch as I scored about a dozen, and he enthralled everybody with his strokeplay. Nobody was more enthralled than I. I recall getting out to the last ball of the morning when I totally mis-read Fleetwood-Smith's spin. I thought I had done well enough to stay there in the shadow of Bradman's skill, but was not allowed to bask in any glory in the dressing room. 'I thought I told you to stay there until lunch,' was Kippax's greeting. Bradman went on to be 187 not out.

As a bowler, the McGilvray experience of that first match was also told with some relish, and always commanded a riveted audience. Had things worked out differently, it might even have set the young McGilvray up for the 1934 tour of England; though he was mentioned for this tour, missing it was never something Alan lamented, since he considered that not making the team allowed his broadcasting career to prosper. The extract, again, is from The Game Is Not The Same.

For more years than most can remember Mac made the Lord Dudley Hotel his home away from home.

ALAN McGILVRAY

Kippax had lost the toss and we were in the field. It was a hot, oppressive day, and as I headed off for a fielding position somewhere about square leg, I reflected on what I considered to be a long, hard job ahead. I looked forward to watching events unfold from the relative obscurity of the field.

'Where do you think you're going?' Kippax inquired. Before I had a chance to reply he thrust the new ball into my hand. 'Take this,' he demanded. 'You're opening the bowling.'

If my knees started to wobble then, they were jelly by the time I turned towards the Jolimont end and saw the lordly figures of Bill Ponsford and Bill Woodfull ambling towards the wicket. These men were giants to me, legends in their own time. My mind retreated to those days back at the SCG when my brother and I, with our packed lunches, stuck our heads between the pickets and ogled their excellence. Now here I was, with a ball in my hand, waiting to bowl to them. I felt much as King Louis, last of the Capets, must have felt as he awaited the guillotine.

'Please God,' I prayed. 'Let me land it on the pitch.' I had this mortal fear that I could not possibly control the ball in the presence of such cricketing aristocracy. I still considered myself rather unworthy of my place among these men.

I reasoned that I would bowl an inswinger first up, not because I thought it would provide any better result but because I felt I had better control over it than I did the outswinger. These men had shown much courage against bowlers of the calibre of England's Harold Larwood. Ponsford was tough, battle hardened, and Woodfull, the Australian captain, was an absolutely prolific batsman. Positive though I was determined to be, I knew there was nothing much in the McGilvray armament to strike fear into their hearts. In the end I abandoned thoughts of bowling the inswinger, too. Better to play safe, I thought. Just bowl straight; just let it land on the pitch.

Ponsford took strike to that first ball. It moved a little in the air, then for some reason jagged off the pitch to whip inside his bat. Ponsford had come forward to drive and, as was his habit so often when he was driving, he got to the pitch of the ball and moved with the shot, leaving his crease in the process. As the ball zipped past the bat Bert Oldfield, who was standing up over the wicket, threw his hands into the air, expecting the ball to hit the stumps. It just missed. By the time Bertie retrieved the ball, the stumping chance was gone too. But I had bowled it straight, and my confidence suddenly took a marvellous turn for the better.

If in every life there is one decisive moment in which its direction is changed forever, one cataclysmic event that irreversibly shapes the future, I imagine that moment came for me in that very first over I bowled in Sheffield Shield cricket.

By the third delivery the batsman had scored a single, and the bulky figure of Woodfull was on strike, standing there like the Rock of Gibraltar, defying any intrusion into his domain. By this time, I had gathered enough confidence to have a go at an inswinger. Woodfull hit it, Oldfield caught it, threw it into the air, and joined in the loud appeal that seemed to come from all points of the compass. To me it was an absolute crescendo echoing around the MCG. Woodfull, caught Oldfield, bowled McGilvray, for nought, and in my first over in first class cricket! What a moment!

'Not out' came the judgment from George Hele, the No 1 umpire of the day and as upstanding a gentleman as ever graced the game. Umpires' opinions were generally respected in those days. Certainly the code of behaviour was very different to that of recent times, when it seems an irreverent mouthful is pretty much part of the game.

I felt no particular disappointment about that decision. I was happy enough to have bowled usefully in the eyes of my teammates.

At the end of the over I approached Woodfull, somewhat gingerly. 'I'm sorry about that appeal, Mr Woodfull,' I offered, much as a schoolboy might have approached his headmaster in confessing a minor misdemeanour.

Woodfull looked straight past me to George Hele. 'Hey George,' he said. 'I hit that hard. I was ready to walk when you called "not out". I stayed there because I didn't want to offend you.'

It was typical of Woodfull to go to such lengths to avoid offence. He didn't throw his wicket away thereafter, mind you, to even things up. But he was very sporting about it, and even if I didn't get the result, I did glean much satisfaction from the knowledge of what might have been.

For all his celebrity and his vast network of friends, it could also be said of Alan McGilvray that he was an essentially private person, for whom the values of home and family were paramount. McGilvray gave the impression that he never really understood the impact his work had on the Australian populus. He was engrossed in his cricket and extremely professional about his broadcasting, determined to make his broadcasts 'breathe' as he put it, so that the listeners not only were totally informed and entertained, but actually a part of the broadcast. He always wanted to make them feel that he was there with them in their homes, talking to them personally. It was no mean feat that he actually went a long way towards achieving that. When he died so many people rang the ABC to make that very point ... that he indeed had been part of their lives, that he had created a bond with his listeners that was very real.

McGilvray would have been quite amazed to have heard such things. Broadcasting cricket was a job of work that he loved, but it

Mac with his children Ross and Carolyn at the Lord Mayor's reception, October 1985.

was a job of work, no different in his eyes from the man who delivered the bread, or the conductor who collected fares on the tram. The impact his work had certainly in no way affected the persona to which he had grown. He was devoted to his family, loved to potter in his garden, enjoyed a drink at the local with his neighbourhood mates.

Alan was devastated when his wife Gwen died in 1976. She had been a great support to him, and Mac put in some hard years after her passing. But his work and his family gave him strength. He was always a picture of delight when his daughter Carolyn joined him on tour, or his son Ross was in town for a Sydney Test. He spoke of his grandchildren with great pride; when he was the subject of a *This Is Your Life* television production in 1979, the tears rolled down his face as his family and the friends of a lifetime were on hand to surprise him.

Mac's Double Bay flat was also an important part of his life. It opened on to a garden in which he grew the most exotic roses. He treated his roses as a collector might treat rare stamps. He dabbled in new strains and when a particularly striking bloom appeared it was like a birth in the family. He had fashioned handles for his kitchen cupboards out of ancient, exquisitely polished British coins, some of which had Queen Victoria's image on them. His MBE and his AM were displayed proudly, and presentations from cricket authorities all over the world adorned his walls and his trophy cabinet.

I was privileged to spend many long hours in that unit working with Alan on the books he wrote in the final year of his broadcasting career, and then in the years that followed. As an author he was a meticulous operator. He would sit in the sun at his desk by the window and pore for hours over old notes, old books, old tapes. He was a remarkable collector of material. Notes he had written in the quiet of night, going back decades, were there for the turning up, yellowed and tattered but certainly useful. Every one of them seemed to open another corner of the McGilvray mind, unearthing a new story, a new revelation. When he had his subject satisfactorily researched, he would then sit at his tape recorder and tell it as he felt it. I ended up with dozens and dozens of those tapes, which I would transcribe and edit, and then massage the words to produce the final product. Then Alan would go over the written version, making sure that it was right; making sure that it was fair; making sure that it would not give offence. The first of the books, *The Game Is Not The Same*, was a best seller that went into six printings over three years. It was a further reflection of the esteem in which McGilvray was held, and of the power of his work in typifying a grand sporting age.

Through all of his work, broadcasting and books, McGilvray was a stickler for standards. He so admired the mentors of his youth, particularly his first Shield captain Alan Kippax, whose meticulous standards of dress and bearing had an enormous influence on him. Mac saw cricket as something more than just a game; it was a way of life, and it encompassed standards of fair play, of respect for your fellow man and of common courtesy and dignity which he saw as a very bulwark of our civilisation. He didn't have much time for modern trends ... sloppy dress and behaviour, 'sledging', disrespect for authority, particularly umpires, and for opponents. In short, he thought many modern players did not treat the game with the reverence it required, and it hurt him. But he did not let that affect his judgment of their cricket. He marvelled at the skills of modern cricketers, and was never one to decry their abilities in favour of previous generations. Rather, he applied the logic that has seen sportsmen and women in every endeavour improve in every way. It was never logical to McGilvray that cricketers could stand apart from swimmers and athletes and golfers and tennis players and the rest, all of whom perform measurably better with modern conditioning, technology, diet and preparation than was the case in generations past.

As times changed and perceptions changed—and sport always has seemed to provide a marked reflection of our society's changing mores—McGilvray compromised nothing in his work. His determination to maintain standards of accuracy and fair play never wavered, no matter how much modern pressures seemed to demand a 'show' from its broadcasters. As such McGilvray became a constant, a tie with more relaxed and more comfortable times, when cricket on the radio was a part of everything we did.

Many things conspired to set Alan McGilvray on his path to being so pre-eminent in his field. His early problems with speech—he was a chronic stutterer—encouraged long hours with an elocutionist, where he developed those wonderfully rounded tones that eventually became as much a part of Australian summers as the cicadas in the trees. At Sydney Grammar School he first encountered the great MA Noble, who encouraged his cricket, formed a friendship with him and eventually was the man who recommended him to then ABC sporting director Charles Moses for trial as a pioneer commentator. McGilvray took to it immediately, developed his own style, pioneered the pure art of ball-by-ball commentary, and for 50 years won himself an indelible place in the history of Australia.

Mac's family became used to Christmas without him. In 1985, however, the whole family was able to get together for the first time in many years. Above: Mac with his children, Ross and Carolyn. Below: Mac with his grandchildren—back row: Andrew, Catriona and Fiona, front row: Sarah, Mac, Kirsty and Angus.

The respect which McGilvray commanded from generations of cricket players, and from literally millions of Australians who had grown up listening to him, was simply unique. In the modern age of proliferating communication, so pivotal a role is no longer possible. The game, indeed, is not the same without McGilvray.